The
Christian's
Bill of Rights

The
Christian's
Bill *of* Rights

A 31-Day Devotional to Help You Live Free

STEVEN J. CAMPBELL

Books for the Harvest
Farmington, New Mexico

The Christian's Bill of Rights

© 2012 by Steven J. Campbell

Author grants permission for any non-commercial reproduction to promote the Kingdom of God.

All other rights reserved.

Published by
Books for the Harvest
Farmington, New Mexico

ISBN-13: 978-0615694498
ISBN-10: 0615694497

Revised Printing—January 2016

Cover Design by Austin J. Campbell

Acknowledgments

I want to acknowledge the fact that I am the product of the influence of many others. First, I have been primarily influenced by the Word of God—the Bible. As I have read and meditated on it, the Bible has shaped my life more than anything else has. Through my personal study, as well as through reading and hearing what others have said, the Holy Spirit has made the Word of God come alive in my life. Therefore, I first acknowledge the Holy Spirit as having the greatest influence in my life—leading me to the love of the Father and to salvation through Jesus Christ.

Also, I want to acknowledge my family, friends, colleagues, other authors, ministers, and churches. All of you have shaped me as a person and as an author. Even though I am not able to acknowledge each one individually, I do want to thank a few people who made this book possible:

> Susan, my wife—who encouraged me to begin to write even when I thought I could not. Her influence in my life is beyond measure.

> Our eight children—each one of you helped me to understand the love of the Heavenly Father better. I want to give a special thanks to Austin, my son, for designing the new cover.

> Finally, I thank all of the unnamed family, friends, colleagues, authors, ministers, and churches for their influence in my life—you have helped make me the person I am.

Table of Contents

Introduction

Deep in the heart of humanity is a cry—a cry for freedom. Even so, is true freedom possible? Yes it is! No matter where you are in life, there is hope for you—the hope for freedom in Jesus Christ. Therefore, I believe the Holy Spirit had me write this book for you, the Christian reader, to help you live more abundantly in what Jesus purchased for you on the cross. That is, on the cross Jesus set you free to follow Him by giving you certain rights for living in freedom.

We find all of these rights in the greatest book ever written—the Bible. These rights are "hidden in plain sight" within its pages. In this book, *The Christian's Bill of Rights,* I have only explored some of these rights for you. Even so, my hope is that this book will encourage you to search out more of your rights that are easily found in the pages of the Holy Scriptures.

Also, in reading this book, you can see how well you are progressing in the basic freedoms Christ has given you. Additionally, as a laborer in the harvest, you can use this book as a tool for helping those you lead to the Lord, which is also my hope for this book—that it will be one of the many tools used in the Great Harvest.

The Great Harvest

The thing of greatest concern in the writing of this book was the harvest that is upon us—one billion people will be born again in a short time. Most of these will be young people, which will need help from established Christians to teach them all that Jesus commanded. This may be the most important reason for writing this book—to help teach new believers in Christ.

When speaking of the harvest, the first thing Jesus said was to pray for laborers. As established Christians, we are to be laborers in this harvest, which Jesus calls "plentiful" (great). *"The harvest truly is plentiful . . ." (Matthew 9:37)*.

Remember fellow laborers, Jesus did not just say to make converts, but to make disciples. Disciples are taught to observe *all* things that Jesus commanded. Jesus' commission for us is: *"Go therefore and make disciples . . . teaching them to observe all things that I have commanded you . . ."* (Matthew 28:19–20).

The Great Harvest is not far off; it is even now in the beginning stages and this book may be used as a simple tool to teach the new Christians some of the basics of following Jesus. Consequently, this book is for the laborers as well as the new believers in Christ.

For the New Believers

If you are a new believer in Christ, this book is for you. As a new believer, you may not be familiar with the teachings of Jesus; therefore, I have included numerous verses from God's Word to confirm to your heart the truth of the rights Jesus gives you. The many Scriptures included will fan the flame in your heart to know all you can about God's Word, and the more you know the Bible's teachings, the better off you will be. Also, your faith will grow as Romans 10:17 states, *"So then faith comes by hearing, and hearing by the word of God."* As a new Christian, you can "jump-start" your faith with the included Bible verses.

Finally, John 8:32 states, *"And you shall know the truth, and the truth shall make you free."* Hence, the subtitle of this book, *A 31-Day Devotional to Help You Live Free.*

Day 1

The Right to Know

Know Your Rights

As an American, you have certain rights given to you by the Constitution of the United States. Then in 1791, the first ten amendments were added to the Constitution; we call these amendments the *Bill of Rights*. Americans should know the rights given to them by these two documents.

As a Christian, you have certain rights given to you in your "Christian Constitution"—the Holy Bible. The Bible is where we find the rights of a Christian. In this book, *The Christian's Bill of Rights,* we will explore some of the rights given to you within the Bible.

Do you know your Christian rights? You have a right to know your rights! The knowledge of your rights is very important as Hosea 4:6 states, *"My people are ruined because they don't know what's right or true" (TMSG).*

What it Means to Have a Right

To have a *right* means to have the freedom to do something, or to have a claim or entitlement to something. God has given us many rights in the Bible. The purpose of this book is not to list all of our rights, but to point out some of our basic Christian rights. In other words, there are more rights not covered in this book than are covered. And the rights I do deal with are not treated in an in-depth manner but in a concise manner to be suitable for a 31-day devotional.

The Basis for Our Christian Rights

I want to make sure we have all of our Christian rights based upon the Bible; consequently, I will quote chapter and verse for almost everything I write in this book. Stated another way, the reason we have all of our Christian rights is because the Bible says we have those rights; therefore, the most important thing in this book is what the Scriptures say. For that reason, a considerable portion of this book is the Scriptures themselves.

So how did we get our Christian rights? God the Father paid for our rights when He purchased us by Jesus Christ; thus, we have certain God-purchased-rights. Acts 20:28 declares, "*. . . the church of God which He purchased with His own blood.*"

Since God purchased us, He wants us to submit ourselves to Him, enjoy the rights He has given to us, and not be "slaves" of men—because men will often try to rob us of our God given rights. *"You were bought at a price; do not become slaves of men" (1 Corinthians 7:23).* God gives us the right not to be slaves of men but to submit ourselves to Him since we are no longer our own—we are purchased with His own blood.

Why Did God Give Us Our Rights?

First, we see that Jesus Christ gave us our rights (liberties, freedoms) so we do not have to be in bondage:

> *Stand fast therefore in the liberty by which Christ has made us free, and do not be entangled again with a yoke of bondage. (Galatians 5:1)*

Second, God gave us our rights so He could redeem our lives from our aimless (directionless) conduct. That is, our Christian rights give direction to our lives:

> *Knowing that you were not redeemed with corruptible things, like silver or gold, from your aimless conduct received by tradition from your fathers, but with the precious blood of Christ . . . (1 Peter 1:18–19)*

Third, our rights enable us to live honorable lives before men and before God—to be good citizens that bring glory to Him. We can do this by honoring everyone including the king (the President) as 1 Peter 2:12–17 states:

> *Having your conduct honorable among the Gentiles, that when they speak against you as evil-doers, they may, by your good works which they observe, glorify God in the day of visitation. Therefore submit yourselves to every ordinance of man for the Lord's sake, whether to the king as supreme, or to governors, as to those who are sent by him for the punishment of evildoers and for the praise of those who do good. For this is the will of God, that by doing good you may put to silence the ignorance of foolish men—as free, yet not using liberty as a cloak for vice, but as bondservants of God. Honor all people. Love the brotherhood. Fear God. Honor the king.*

Finally, the supreme reason God gives us our Christian rights is so that we can serve others in love. God is love and our rights free us to be like Him (love is the thing most like Him). Therefore, there is no greater reason for our rights than for loving God and loving others. That is to say, God has called us to use our Christian rights to serve others through love:

> *For you, brethren, have been called to liberty; only do not use liberty as an opportunity for the flesh, but through love serve one another. (Galatians 5:13)*

Indeed, our supreme right is to receive love and to love (as we will see in the next chapter).

The Right to Be So Loved and to Love

We Are So Loved

God does not just love us; He **so** loves us! The love of the Father is *so* great that He established a special period of time and a very special way to reveal it:

> *The stone the builders rejected has become the capstone . . . This is the day the LORD has made, let us rejoice and be glad in it. (Psalms 118:22–24 NIV)*

The day the Lord made to show forth His great love is the day(s) of Jesus' sufferings, death, and His resurrection—what Jesus did shows the depth of God's love for us. Jesus **is** the very expression of God's love. He *so* loved the Father that He wanted to express to all of creation the depth of love that the Father possesses. Therefore, He came to earth, suffered, and died for us, showing the magnificent love of the Father.

> *For God so loved the world that He gave His only begotten Son, that whoever believes in Him should not perish but have everlasting life. (John 3:16)*

Believing in what Jesus did for us gives us the right to be loved so much by Father God and to be with Him forever!

Being Loved Is First

Our love for God is born out of His love for us; therefore, we would not love Him if He did not first love us. The Scripture shows that He loved us before we loved Him. *"We love Him because He first loved us" (1 John 4:19).*

Love is the nature of God, and *all* love originates in God. The Bible says it best; *"God is love" (1 John 4:8).* This is the key to all of our love; that is, being loved by God sets the foundation for our love. In fact, we must *be loved* before we can truly love others. Because God first so loved us, we can so love others. To say it another way, to the degree that we have received the love of God to that degree we can love others. Because of this, Christians should have more love than unbelievers have. As the Scripture says, *"By this all will know that you are My disciples, if you have love for one another" (John 14:35).*

Without a doubt, we need to experience the love of God for our own sake and for the sake of those who need our love.

The Apostle John seems to have experienced the love of God as much as any of the other apostles did and he shows us in 1 John how the Father's love for us should affect our relationships—*"Beloved, if God so loved us, we also ought to love one another" (1 John 4:11).*

Then in 1 John 4:20–21, he continues to show us that there is a direct connection between loving God and loving others:

> *If someone says, "I love God," and hates his brother, he is a liar; for he who does not love his brother whom he has seen, how can he love*

God whom he has not seen? And this commandment we have from Him: that he who loves God must love his brother also.

To Be So Loving

The Christian life is a growth. We grow in our love for God and our love for one another. We all need to keep growing in love; and the best way to grow in love is to keep receiving God's love. The more of His love we receive into our hearts, the more love we have to give. Thus, we have the right to be *so* loving of others because God *so* loves us.

God gave us Jesus Christ as the perfect example of loving others—*"Greater love has no one than this, than to lay down one's life for his friends" (John 15:13).*

In the next chapter, we will look at a basic example of growing in love.

The Right to Be Forgiven and to Forgive

The Right to Receive Forgiveness

Forgiveness is from God through Jesus Christ by His shed blood; therefore, we can never earn God's forgiveness for our sins. God's total forgiveness and cleansing of our sins is only through His Son Jesus Christ—His blood cleanses our sins. *". . . and without the shedding of blood there is no forgiveness" (Hebrews 9:22 NIV).*

One *very* important aspect of Jesus' cleansing blood is the cleansing of our conscience from dead works. Dead works are *our works* that we try to use to impress God or to earn His forgiveness. However, God has already accomplished the work for our forgiveness. Thus, our working for His forgiveness does not impress Him; it actually displeases Him since Jesus is the One who paid the high price for our forgiveness.

We all need our conscience cleansed from trying to earn God's forgiveness; in fact, it's very prideful to think that we could pay the price for our own sins when it took the sinless Lamb of God (Jesus) giving His life's blood to forgive our sins. *"How much more shall the blood of Christ . . . cleanse your conscience from dead works to serve the living God?" (Hebrews 9:14).*

The Scriptures tell us that God the Father is the One who gives us the right (qualifies us) to be forgiven through His Son:

Giving thanks to the Father who has qualified us to be partakers of the inheritance of the saints in the light. ... in whom we have redemption through His blood, the forgiveness of sins. (Colossians 1:12–14)

God Does Not Want Us Living in Sin

God does not want us to sin; however, when we do sin, He wants us to confess our sin to Him and then believe that He forgives us and cleanses us from the sin. Nevertheless, we are not to be constantly sinning, for that would be walking in darkness instead of walking in His light as 1 John 1:6–9 shows:

If we claim to have fellowship with him yet walk in the darkness, we lie and do not live by the truth. But if we walk in the light, as he is in the light, we have fellowship with one another, and the blood of Jesus, his Son, purifies us from all sin. If we claim to be without sin, we deceive ourselves and the truth is not in us. If we confess our sins, he is faithful and just and will forgive us our sins and purify us from all unrighteousness. (NIV)

To continue **living** in sin demonstrates that we have never been born of God—it shows that we do not know Him. The Scriptures are very aggressive when speaking about anyone continuing in sin.

Now by this we know that we know Him, if we keep His commandments. He who says, "I know Him," and does not keep His commandments, is a liar, and the truth is not in him. (1 John 2:3–4)

In addition to this, the Scriptures say in 1 John 3:6–9:

No one who lives in him keeps on sinning. No one who continues to sin has either seen him or known him. Dear children, do not let anyone lead you astray. He who does what is right is righteous, just as he [Jesus] is righteous. He who does what is sinful is of the devil, because the devil has been sinning from the beginning. The reason the Son of God appeared was to destroy the devil's work. No one who is born of God will continue to sin, because God's seed remains in him; he cannot go on sinning, because he has been born of God. (NIV)

God's Forgiveness Is Linked with Our Forgiveness

God's forgiveness is based upon Jesus' finished work; nevertheless, our forgiveness of others determines God's forgiveness of our sins. This is a *most important* aspect of forgiveness to understand—if we do not forgive others, we will not be forgiven! It is necessary for us to understand this fact because family, friends, neighbors, associates, or even other Christians have sinned against us; and when we do not forgive *every* trespass against us, it can cause us physical, mental, and emotional damage. Yet, the worst result is the lack of forgiveness from God for our own sins.

A prayer most of us have prayed is the "Lord's Prayer" of Matthew 6:12, *"And forgive us our sins, as we have forgiven those who have sinned against us"* (ISV). At the end of this prayer, Jesus again emphasizes this most important point:

> *For if you forgive men when they sin against you, your heavenly Father will also forgive you. But if you do not forgive men their sins, your Father will not forgive your sins. (Matthew 6:14–15 NIV).*

That verse raises the next question, "How often should we forgive someone who sins against us?" Jesus spoke directly to this question in Matthew 18:21–22:

> *Then Peter came to Him and said, "Lord, how often shall my brother sin against me, and I forgive him? Up to seven times?" Jesus said to him, "I do not say to you, up to seven times, but up to seventy times seven."*

What happens if we decide not to forgive? Jesus gives a parable letting us know what happens when we do not forgive (see Matthew 18:23–35). At the end of that chapter, Jesus says:

> *"Should you not also have had compassion on your fellow servant, just as I had pity on you?" And his master was angry, and delivered him to the torturers until he should pay all that was due to him. "So My heavenly Father also will do to you if each of you, from his heart, does not forgive his brother his trespasses." (Matthew 18:33–35)*

Don't Forget Yourself

When God forgives us and we forgive the person who sinned against us, there is still one more person to forgive—we must forgive ourselves! Sometimes forgiving ourselves is one of the hardest things to do. Therefore, the question is, "If I sin, do I forgive myself?"

We can forgive ourselves because God forgives us. To say it another way, we know we are worthy of forgiveness because God says that *He* forgives us based upon what Jesus did for us on the cross. So let's never forget about forgiving ourselves!

Learning to Forgive

Total forgiveness is God's requirement; however, we *learn* to forgive. Forgiveness does not come naturally to us; it comes "super-naturally" to us; it originates in us by the Holy Spirit because of God's forgiveness. He knows that we must *learn* to yield to the forgiveness that He wants to place in our hearts. Could this be a reason why we have so many opportunities to forgive ourselves, and others—so we learn forgiveness? Probably so, for without a doubt, forgiveness is a *major* sign of maturing in love, which is God's central desire for our lives—mature love.

Our Rights

We have the right to receive forgiveness for all of our sins, and we have the right to give forgiveness to everyone who sins against us. These two fundamental rights are purchased for us by Jesus Christ. Let's make sure we walk in both of these rights.

The Right to Be Free from Shame

The Origin of Shame

The first awareness Adam and Eve had after disobeying God was their nakedness. And what did they do about it? They covered their nakedness. Why? Because they were ashamed of themselves since they now needed to be clothed. That is, they needed their shame (sin) before God to be covered.

The book of Genesis states, *"And the* LORD *God commanded the man, saying, '. . . of the tree of the knowledge of good and evil you shall not eat, for in the day that you eat of it you shall surely die'"* (Genesis 2:17).

However, Adam and Eve chose to disobey God:

> *So when the woman saw that the tree was good for food . . . she took of its fruit and ate. She also gave to her husband with her, and he ate. Then the eyes of both of them were opened, and they knew that they were naked; and they sewed fig leaves together and made themselves coverings. . . . Then the* LORD *God called to Adam and said to him, "Where are you?" So he said, "I heard Your voice in the garden, and I was afraid because I was naked; and I hid myself."* (Genesis 3:6–10)

The only remedy for our sin and shame is to have God clothe us. Our coverings of our nakedness (our sinful condition) will never remove our shame, which is one reason why God clothed Adam and Eve—to remove their shame. *"Also for Adam and his wife the LORD God made tunics of skin, and clothed them" (Genesis 3:21).*

What Is Shame?

Shame is a negative emotion that brings us strong feelings of dishonor, embarrassment, or unworthiness. Shame causes strong feelings of regret or disappointment from doing something wrong or of not doing something right (sins of commission or sins of omission). Shame is being in a state of disgrace.

Shame Is Against Grace

Shame is a disgrace since it is "dis-grace"—meaning "lack of grace" or "opposite of grace." Shame hinders us from receiving God's grace. When God forgives our sin, there is no need for us to feel one bit of shame about it no matter what we have done, since Jesus defeated sin and shame on the cross! That statement is worth repeating again in slightly different words—Jesus took away our sins *and shame* on the cross; therefore we have the right to be free of *all* shame so that we can receive His grace.

Jesus' Attitude Concerning Shame

Jesus despises shame and thinks of it with contempt because He was put to an open shame on the cross. Even though Jesus despised the shame of the cross, He endured it with joy knowing that He was setting us free from sin *and shame* and that He was about to sit down at the right hand of God—the place of authority—authority over shame forever!

Looking unto Jesus, the author and finisher of our faith, who for the joy that was set before Him endured the cross, despising the shame, and has sat down at the right hand of the throne of God. (Hebrews 12:2)

The meaning of the word translated as *despising* in the above verse is: to think of with contempt or scorn, to despise or to distain, to refuse or reject something as wrong or disgraceful. To say it another way, Jesus absolutely despises shame because it hinders His children from freely receiving His grace. That is, shame can hinder us from coming with confidence before His throne of grace.

> *Let us then approach the throne of grace with confidence, so that we may receive mercy and find grace to help us in our time of need. (Hebrews 4:16 NIV)*

Knowing what Jesus thinks about shame, we may decide not to say to others, "Shame on you!"

Shame Is Equated with Being Unclothed

We need Jesus to clothe our nakedness so we will not be ashamed:

> *. . . you say, "I am rich, have become wealthy, and have need of nothing"—and do not know that you are wretched, miserable, poor, blind, and naked—I counsel you to buy from Me . . . white garments, that you may be clothed, that the shame of your nakedness may not be revealed. (Revelation 3:17–18)*

Jesus says that our nakedness (our current condition) is our shame. Therefore, He counsels us to buy our "clothes" from Him so we can truly have our nakedness covered. Until we are clothed with Christ's salvation, shame will remain.

Don't Live with Shame

God does not want His children living with shame. He wants us clothed with His grace, not clothed in the disgrace of shame. For that reason, we should not let shame keep us from quickly confessing our sins and receiving His forgiveness through the work of His cross. Through the cross, He took away our shame so we could be free—free to receive all His grace and mercy. Freedom from shame is our Christian right!

The Right to Be Holy

Two Types of Holiness

There are two types of holiness—a holiness *before men* and a holiness *before God*. Some, if not most, only think of holiness as the one type—holiness before men. We have the right **not** to be holy before men! Instead, we have the right to be holy before God. As stated previously, there is holiness unto men and there is holiness unto God as Colossians 2:20–23 states:

> *Therefore, if you died with Christ from the basic principles of the world, why, as though living in the world, do you subject yourselves to regulations—"Do not touch, do not taste, do not handle," which all concern things which perish with the using—according to the commandments and doctrines of men? These things indeed have an appearance of wisdom in self-imposed religion, false humility, and neglect of the body, but are of no value against the indulgence of the flesh.*

Many have a very negative attitude concerning holiness because God did not create us for living under the commandments and doctrines of men to be holy. Yes, these "rules" have an appearance of religious wisdom, but they are of no value in stopping sinful behavior. As a result, when we try to live under the commandments and doctrines of men, we find that we are not able to live up to their idealistic standards. Then our failure with this so-called holiness causes an aversion for all holiness.

The Right to Be Holy

God created man to be holy *unto Him*. Therefore, we have a right to be holy because of His holiness. *"Because it is written, 'Be holy, for I am holy'" (1 Peter 1:16).* God wants us to be like Him; since He is holy, we have a right to be holy.

What Is Holiness?

What does it mean to be holy? It simply means to be set apart or dedicated unto God. The Apostle Peter said in 1 Peter 1:15, *"But as He who called you is holy, you also be holy in all your conduct."* Therefore, all of our conduct ought to be pleasing to God since we are set apart or dedicated unto Him. In other words, all aspects of our lives are to be dedicated to pleasing God, which is true holiness.

True holiness comes from God. God is love; therefore, love is the starting point for holiness, which is why Jesus said in John 14:15, *"If you love Me, keep My commandments."* Thus, we see that Jesus wants our holiness based upon our love for Him—because love is the *foundation* for true holiness. This foundation is an unmovable foundation because our love for God is based upon His love for us. *"We love Him because He first loved us" (1 John 4:19).*

The foundation for our holiness is God's love for us; then we build upon it with our love for Him. Because of this, our holiness comes from our heart's desire to please God since He loves us so much. Therefore, our holiness is not just an outward show for others; it is an inward and outward expression of our love for God.

The Importance of Holiness

The Word of God is called the *Holy* Bible or the *Holy* Book. The Spirit of God is called the *Holy* Spirit. Plus, the Scriptures call God the Father and His son Jesus Christ, *Holy*. Since this Holy God made humanity to be with Him as a loving family, we must be holy. Consequently, God says that we will not even see Him if we are not holy. *"Pursue peace with all people, and holiness, without which no one will see the Lord" (Hebrews 12:14).*

In the next chapter, we will look at the fact that it is not about our strength but about Jesus' strength in our lives to be what He wants us to be—like Him (see Matthew 5:48).

Day 6

The Right to Be Weak and Strong

Weakness and Strength

Why would we ever want the right to be weak? Why would anyone want to admit to his or her weaknesses? Who would ever boast in their weaknesses? Should we do all we can to hide our weaknesses? Does it disappoint God when we have weaknesses?

God answers these great questions for us in the Scriptures. But before we look at the answers, I will set some groundwork.

We have been taught from the time we were young not to be weak. Is there anything wrong with that? The answer is two-fold. The first answer is, "No"—because God wants us to be strong. The second answer is, "Yes"—because He wants us to be strong in Him and not in our own power. *"Finally, my brethren, be strong in the Lord and in the power of His might." (Ephesians 6:10).* God does not want us to think that it is by our own power that we overcome the things of this world; it's our faith in Him that gives us the power to overcome. *"For whatever is born of God overcomes the world. And this is the victory that has overcome the world—our faith" (1 John 5:4).*

The Power of Weakness

God wants us mature and strong, but the danger is that we can easily begin to trust more in our own strength than in His strength. Most would agree that the Apostle Paul was a very strong Christian—since he had a very strong faith in Jesus' power in his life. However, Jesus had to confront Paul directly on the issue of his weaknesses. Paul wanted to be strong for Jesus, but he did not fully understand the power and strength of his own weaknesses. Therefore, Jesus spoke plainly to him about his weaknesses as 2 Corinthians 12:9–10 states:

> *And then he told me, My grace is enough; it's all you need. My strength comes into its own in your weakness. Once I heard that, I was glad to let it happen. I quit focusing on the handicap and began appreciating the gift. It was a case of Christ's strength moving in on my weakness. Now I take limitations in stride, and with good cheer, these limitations that cut me down to size—abuse, accidents, opposition, bad breaks. I just let Christ take over! And so the weaker I get, the stronger I become. (TMSG)*

We need to appreciate our weaknesses that keep us "cut down to size," not so that we can be weak, but so that we can be strong *in Him.* As we know, this is not a natural human response to our weaknesses; we prefer to hide our weaknesses. Because of this, we need to know what Jesus thinks about our weaknesses.

Why Weakness?

God's view of our weaknesses is contrary to our natural mind—He knows that our weaknesses give Him opportunity to shine through us, which means people will see His power in us instead of our own strength. If we want others to see the power of Jesus in us, we have to embrace our weaknesses. Since this is such an important principle to learn, I will give Jesus' view of our weaknesses from another translation:

> *But he said to me, "My grace is sufficient for you, for my power is made perfect in weakness." Therefore I will boast all the more gladly about my weaknesses, so that Christ's power may rest on me. That is why, for Christ's sake, I delight in weaknesses, in insults, in hardships, in persecutions, in difficulties. For when I am weak, then I am strong. (2 Corinthians 12:9–10 NIV)*

A major issue in all I have been writing about in this chapter is the glory of God:

> *For you see your calling, brethren, that not many wise according to the flesh, not many mighty, not many noble, are called. But God has chosen . . . the weak things of the world to put to shame the things which are mighty . . . that no flesh should glory in His presence. . . . that, as it is written, "He who glories, let him glory in the Lord." (1 Corinthians 1:26–31)*

We can be strong in our weaknesses. In other words, we have the right to be weak in ourselves so that we can be strong in Him, which gives Him glory.

Day 7

The Right to Be Humble

The Need for Humility

Pride can cost us greatly because we could have the greatest power in the universe resisting us—*God!* If God is resisting us, then we are in the most terrible predicament that we need to find our way out of as fast as possible. The way out would be to humble ourselves because *"God resists the proud, but gives grace to the humble" (1 Peter 5:5).*

We do not want any of God's resistance. It would be better to have the devil and all of his followers resisting us than to have God resisting us. As much as possible, we need God's grace that He gives to the humble. Thus, we should humble ourselves and receive His grace.

What It Means to Be Humble

Having low self-esteem is not humility. Humility believes what God declares about us. So, when God tells us to do something, we should not say that we are not capable because of some weakness that we may have (for God usually chooses those who are weak in something to do the very thing that they are weak in). God calls the weak so that they can trust in Him and not in themselves.

One of the greatest leaders in the Old Testament found out that it angered God when he did not trust Him to do what He told him to do. We see this fact when God told Moses to speak to the king but Moses did not want to speak because he had a speech impediment; so he pleaded with God to send someone else to speak, which angered God.

> *Moses raised another objection to GOD: "Master, please, I don't talk well. I've never been good with words, neither before nor after you spoke to me. I stutter and stammer." GOD said, "And who do you think made the human mouth? And who makes some mute, some deaf, some sighted, some blind? Isn't it I, GOD? So, get going. I'll be right there with you—with your mouth! I'll be right there to teach you what to say." He said, "Oh, Master, please! Send somebody else!" GOD got angry with Moses . . . (Exodus 4:10–15 TMSG)*

God knew that Moses stuttered and stammered when he spoke; even so, God told Moses to speak to the people and to the king because He wanted Moses to be humble enough to trust *Him* to speak through him. He wanted Moses to look beyond his own speaking abilities and to trust in His ability to speak through him.

An Example of Humility

The Apostle Paul is an example of humility. Look at what he said about himself: *"For I am the least of the apostles, who am not worthy to be called an apostle, because I persecuted the church of God" (1 Corinthians 15:9)*. You may think that Paul had low self-esteem, but that is not the case. He knew that he did as much apostolic work as anyone, but it was not by his power, it was by God's grace (power).

But by the grace of God I am what I am, and
His grace toward me was not in vain; but I
labored more abundantly than they all, yet not
I, but the grace of God which was with me.
(1 Corinthians 15:10)

Now let's see what Paul says about himself years later, because there seems to be a progression in his humility from "least of the saints" to "chief of sinners."

This is a faithful saying and worthy of all
acceptance, that Christ Jesus came into the
world to save sinners, of whom I am chief.
However, for this reason I obtained mercy,
that in me first Jesus Christ might show all
longsuffering, as a pattern to those who are
going to believe on Him for everlasting life.
(1 Timothy 1:15–16)

The Scriptures tell us to accept the saying, "Christ Jesus came into the world to save sinners, of whom I am chief." In other words, we are to accept the fact that Paul was chief of sinners and Jesus saved him showing that He, Jesus, can save anyone. According to the Scriptures, this fact is "worthy of all acceptance."

The Supreme Example We Are to Follow

The greatest example of humility is the man Christ Jesus. He set the example of humility for *each* of us:

When the time came, he set aside the privileges
of deity and took on the status of a slave,
became human! Having become human, he
stayed human. It was an incredibly humbling

> *process. He didn't claim special privileges. Instead, he lived a selfless, obedient life and then died a selfless, obedient death—and the worst kind of death at that: a crucifixion. (Philippians 2:7–8 TMSG)*

Jesus is *the example* of humility set for us. He humbled Himself and became human, then further humbled Himself by dying on the cross. Jesus *is* humility! The more we abide in Him, the more humility we will have in our life.

Exaltation Comes After Humility

Look at what happened after Jesus humbled Himself:

> *Therefore God also has highly exalted Him and given Him the name which is above every name, that at the name of Jesus every knee should bow, of those in heaven, and of those on earth, and of those under the earth. (Philippians 2:9–11)*

God says that He will also exalt us if we will humble ourselves. Does that mean that our exaltation is to the degree that we humble ourselves? That seems to be the case—that greater humbling equals greater exaltation. Whatever the case, God does exalt those who humble themselves. *"Therefore humble yourselves under the mighty hand of God, that He may exalt you in due time"* (1 Peter 5:6). Notice that the exaltation is in God's timing.

Humbling Words

The following words of Jesus can also help us to be more humble:

So likewise you, when you have done all those things which you are commanded, say, "We are unprofitable servants. We have done what was our duty to do." (Luke 17:10)

Jesus does not mean for us to just say, *"We are unprofitable servants,"* without believing what we are saying. He wants us to believe in our hearts that we are unprofitable servants simply doing what is our duty to do. In light of this, we need to ask ourselves, "If I do all God wants me to do, will I be able to truly say, 'I am an unprofitable servant just doing my duty,' and mean what I am saying?" Or, "Will I boast in the fact that I did all He commanded me to do?"

When we keep in mind that God loves humility but resists pride, it helps us to humble ourselves every chance we get.

Day 8

The Right to Speak

Communication

We know that God created man for relationship with Him and with one another. For that reason, God gave humanity the ability to speak because our vocal speaking communicates who and what we are to the person we are speaking to. Thus, from the beginning speech was the primary way of building relationships; however, in today's world we have more ways of building relationships with technologies of emailing, texting, and social networking.

Since our communication is important to all of our relationships, we have the right to speak in various ways; for without communication, there can be no true relationship.

The Right to Speak the Truth

God gives us the right to speak the truth. We have this important right even when it is not *politically correct*. However, the Lord does warn us to speak the truth in love since love empowers truth. Truth and love go hand-in-hand. For sure, truth is not complete without love, nor is love complete without truth; therefore, we should always speak the truth in love—*"But, speaking the truth in love, may grow up in all things into Him who is the head—Christ" (Ephesians 4:15).*

Truth spoken in love helps us grow up into Jesus, who is the Truth (see John 14:6). Just as truth needs to be in love, so love needs to be in truth. The Apostle John wrote about this in 1 John 3:18, *"My little children, let us not love in word or in tongue, but in deed and in truth."*

Living our lives in the truth enables us to love other Christians fervently.

> *Since you have purified your souls in obeying the truth through the Spirit in sincere love of the brethren, love one another fervently with a pure heart. (1 Peter 1:22)*

To say it another way, obeying the truth fires up our love for others. An important part of obeying the truth is to speak the truth because God wants our relationships based on truth. *"Therefore, putting away lying, 'Let each one of you speak truth with his neighbor'"* (Ephesians 4:25).

A Dream Come True

Have you ever dreamed about being able to speak with someone you admire? Maybe you have thought about what it would be like to speak with some movie star you admire, or a sports hero, or a singer, or an artist, or a world leader, or the President of the United States. Perhaps you have desired to speak with a world-class religious leader such as a Billy Graham, or the Pope, or the modern-day Mother Teresa—Heidi Baker. Maybe you have even dreamed of speaking with an angel, or perhaps even Gabriel or Michael the archangel. If any of these are your dream, your dream is much too small!

For I have great news for you, the greatest dream you could ever dream is already true—you may speak with God! In fact, as a Christian, you already have the Holy Spirit living within you:

Do you not know that you are the temple of
God and that the Spirit of God dwells in you?
(1 Corinthians 3:16)

Therefore, you can have 24/7 conversation with God!
This is your blood bought right.

The Right to Speak with God

You have the most awesome privilege; you have the
right to speak with the God of the universe! Jesus Himself
encourages you to speak directly to the Heavenly Father
when He says in Matthew 6:6:

But you, when you pray, go into your room,
and when you have shut your door, pray to
your Father who is in the secret place . . .

Jesus wants you to ask the Father in heaven for
things—"*. . . how much more will your Father who is in*
heaven give good things to those who ask him!"
(Matthew 7:11). However, you are to ask the Father for
things in Jesus' name. "*. . . whatever you ask the Father*
in my name, he will give it to you" *(John 15:16 ISV)*.

Jesus promises you that the Father will give you what
you ask in His name since He has given you the right to
speak directly with the Father through Him:

. . . whatever you ask the Father in My name
He will give you. Until now you have asked
nothing in My name. Ask, and you will receive,
that your joy may be full. (John 16:23–24)

There is a fullness of joy in speaking with and receiving
answers from your Father in heaven given that He

answers you out of His love for you—because you love His
Son.

> *In that day you will ask in My name, and I do
> not say to you that I shall pray the Father for
> you; for the Father Himself loves you, because
> you have loved Me . . . (John 16:26–27)*

We will look at another important aspect of our right to
speak in the next chapter.

Day 9

The Right to Be Heard

Why Speak?

Why did God give us the ability to speak? The answer is simple—so we could be heard. Speaking is *just speaking* until someone hears us; at that point, it becomes communication.

God made humans in His image, and since God wants to be heard, humanity wants to be heard. We can see God's desire to be heard because a common phrase of the Old Testament prophet was, *"hear the word of the LORD."* In addition, Jesus spoke to the churches in the book of Revelation several times saying, *"He who has an ear, let him hear what the Spirit says to the churches."*

We all speak with our voices every day and "speak" with our bodily gestures, which is called *body language.* Even those who cannot speak vocally still try to communicate by "speaking" some other way (sign language, gestures, writing, etc.). We willingly exert all this effort to communicate every day because we want to be heard. The good news is that God gives us the right to be heard.

God Hears

God gives us the ability to speak to Him so that He can hear us. Perhaps the greatest privilege in the universe is the fact that we can talk to God and that He listens to us. And He does not just listen, He responds to us as the Apostle John states:

Now this is the confidence that we have in Him, that if we ask anything according to His will, He hears us. And if we know that He hears us, whatever we ask, we know that we have the petitions that we have asked of Him. (1 John 5:14–15)

God wants us to have the confidence that He is hearing us; because without that confidence, we probably will not speak to Him, or at least not very often.

The Consequences of Sin

Sin can block our communication with God; therefore, we need to guard our hearts so that sin does not keep God from hearing us.

But your iniquities have separated between you and your God, and your sins have hid his face from you, that he will not hear. (Isaiah 59:2)

Notice that the words "iniquities" and "sins" are in the plural. The continual sins and iniquities keep God from hearing us, not the one time or occasional sin. We also see this fact in Psalm 66:18:

If I regard iniquity in my heart,
The Lord will not hear.

The "regarding of iniquity" keeps the Lord from hearing us. Another translation paraphrases this word as "cozy with evil."

If I had been cozy with evil, the Lord would never have listened. But he most surely did listen, he came on the double when he heard my prayer. (Psalm 66:18–19 TMSG)

Since the writer of this Psalm was not "cozy with evil," the Lord heard him. Remember, we are *willingly* giving up our right to be heard by God if we allow sin to reign in our lives.

Day 10

The Right to Pray

There Is a Fight Against Prayer

As we all know, in the last few decades there has been an assault against Christian prayer. Prayer has been outlawed in public schools and restricted in many other areas. Sometimes prayer is allowed, but not in Jesus' name. Even the early church had this problem. *"So they called them and commanded them not to speak at all nor teach in the name of Jesus" (Acts 4:18).*

Why is there such a great fight against the prayers of Christians but not against the prayers of people from other religions? Is it because the prayers of Christians have great power with God? Yes, that is why there is such a fight against Christians' prayers—because of what our prayers accomplish, which the devil hates. *"The effective, fervent prayer of a righteous man avails much" (James 5:16).*

When Should We Pray?

We probably all pray when we are suffering, which is encouraged in the Scriptures. *"Is anyone among you suffering? Let him pray" (James 5:13).* However, that should not to be the only time we pray. We are to pray always. That does not mean to pray constantly, or to do nothing except pray. What it does mean is to be in prayer continually as the Holy Spirit directs us. *"Praying always with all prayer and supplication in the Spirit . . ." (Ephesians 6:18).*

Also, we can pray whenever we desire to; in other words, whenever we will to, we can pray. The Apostle Paul prayed in the spirit (in tongues) when he wanted to, and when he wanted to, he prayed with the understanding. *"I will pray with the spirit, and I will also pray with the understanding"* (1 Corinthians 14:15).

Furthermore, whenever we think of those who need to receive Jesus as savior, we should pray. Jesus gave us some instruction in praying for the lost in Luke 10:2:

> *The harvest truly is great, but the laborers are few; therefore pray the Lord of the harvest to send out laborers into His harvest.*

How Should We Pray?

Jesus, the greatest teacher on prayer, taught us some principles on how to pray in Matthew 6:6–13:

> *But when you pray, go into your room, close the door and pray to your Father, who is unseen. Then your Father, who sees what is done in secret, will reward you. And when you pray, do not keep on babbling like pagans, for they think they will be heard because of their many words. Do not be like them, for your Father knows what you need before you ask him.*

> *This then, is how you should pray: Our Father in heaven, hallowed be your name, your kingdom come, your will be done on earth as it is in heaven. Give us today our daily bread. Forgive us our debts, as we also have forgiven*

our debtors. And lead us not into temptation,
but deliver us from the evil one. (NIV)

Notice how Jesus made prayer simple, not complex. By doing this, Jesus showed us that prayer is not some religious exercise; it is simply talking to our Father in heaven. That is, prayer is not for show, but for connection and relationship with God the Father. Even so, your Heavenly Father still wants you to ask Him for the things you need; however, because He already knows your needs, you can keep your requests simple and to the point.

Reasons to Pray

One reason to pray is that we are thankful for what God did and is doing for us—since God is so good to us, we want our prayers filled with thanksgiving. *"Continue earnestly in prayer, being vigilant in it with thanksgiving" (Colossians 4:2).*

Another great reason to pray is for His help so that we do not enter into temptation. *"Watch and pray, lest you enter into temptation. The spirit indeed is willing, but the flesh is weak" (Mark 14:38).*

We also build ourselves up in faith through prayer—especially prayer in the Holy Spirit (tongues). *"But you, beloved, building yourselves up on your most holy faith, praying in the Holy Spirit" (Jude verse 20).*

Also, we pray to receive the things we desire. *"What things soever ye desire, when ye pray, believe that ye receive them, and ye shall have them" (Mark 11:24 KJV).*

In addition, we often desire to pray with others— agreeing with others in prayer is very powerful and special for everyone involved. The Father likes His children to agree in prayer, and when we do, He gives us special promises:

> *Again I say to you that if two of you agree on earth concerning anything that they ask, it will be done for them by My Father in heaven. For where two or three are gathered together in My name, I am there in the midst of them. (Matthew 18:19–20)*

Finally, and most importantly, we pray because of the fellowship we receive with the Father, Son, and Holy Spirit—just wanting to spend time together since we all love each other. That is, prayer is a time of *fellowship with God,* not just a religious exercise.

The Right to Be Free

For This Purpose

Jesus set us free so we could be *free indeed!* That is, our freedom *is* the purpose for Jesus setting us free. To say it in yet another way: Jesus set us free so that we can enjoy the benefits of freedom.

> *It is for freedom that Christ has set us free. Stand firm, then, and do not let yourselves be burdened again by a yoke of slavery. (Galatians 5:1 NIV)*

As we see from this verse, God does not want us under the bondage of the doctrines of men. The Book of Galatians is a key book in expressing our freedom in Christ, so let's look at some of these verses in Galatians:

> *Christ has set us free to live a free life. So take your stand! Never again let anyone put a harness of slavery on you. (Galatians 5:1 TMSG)*

> *When you attempt to live by your own religious plans and projects, you are cut off from Christ, you fall out of grace. (Galatians 5:4 TMSG)*

> *For in Christ, neither our most conscientious religion nor disregard of religion amounts to anything. What matters is something far more*

interior: faith expressed in love. (Galatians 5:6 TMSG)

Faith in God's work sets us free; however, when we trust in our works, we are in bondage to our performance, which results in the constant burden of trying to do more to please God and men.

Love and Freedom

True freedom is faith in God's finished work, which enables us to love God and to love others—love takes precedent over our freedom. That is why we should not use our freedom when it harms another. *"But be careful that by using your freedom you don't somehow make a believer who is weak in faith fall into sin"* (1 Corinthians 8:9 GW).

Again, we see this important point of love's relation to freedom in Galatians 5:13:

> *It is absolutely clear that God has called you to a free life. Just make sure that you don't use this freedom as an excuse to do whatever you want to do and destroy your freedom. Rather, use your freedom to serve one another in love; that's how freedom grows. (TMSG)*

True freedom is found when we walk in love; but if we use our freedom as a license to do whatever we want, we will never find true freedom. The path of true freedom is walking in love!

The Deep Desire for Freedom

The desire for freedom is very deep within the heart of humans. It was the desire for freedom that birthed the

United States of America. Many, if not most who originally came to America, came for freedom—especially religious freedom. To expound on this deep desire for freedom, we will look at how deep that desire went in one of the Founding Fathers—Patrick Henry. On March 23, 1775, at St. John's Church in Richmond, Virginia, Patrick Henry is credited with saying the following words in his speech:

> Is life so dear, or peace so sweet, as to be purchased at the price of chains and slavery? Forbid it, Almighty God! I know not what course others may take; but for me, give me liberty, or give me death!

We should never apologize for our deep desire for freedom because God gave us that deep desire that can only be entirely fulfilled through receiving what Jesus did for us.

> *But now having been set free from sin, and having become slaves of God, you have your fruit to holiness, and the end, everlasting life. (Romans 6:22).*

Being a slave of God is the greatest freedom! This fact will only be understood as we experience it. For Jesus sets us free indeed—free to love God and love one another.

Day 12

The Right to Sacrifice

The Example to Follow

God's sacrifice is the basis for our sacrifices; He set the example for us to follow—the Father and Son sacrificing their best because of their love for us. God desires that we imitate Him in living sacrificially—to be motivated by our love for Him and our love for others. *"Therefore be imitators of God as dear children. And walk in love, as Christ also has loved us . . . (Ephesians 5:1–2).*

Our Sacrificial Service

God even pleads with us to present ourselves as a living sacrifice:

> *I beseech you therefore, brethren, by the mercies of God, that you present your bodies a living sacrifice, holy, acceptable to God, which is your reasonable service. (Romans 12:1)*

Notice that our sacrificial living is acceptable *unto God,* which makes it reasonable. That is to say, God is very reasonable in the sacrificial service He requires of us. If we think His requirements are unreasonable, it is because we have not seen them from God's eternal perspective.

> *For I consider that the sufferings of this present time are not worthy to be compared with the glory which shall be revealed in us. (Romans 8:18)*

The cross is the ultimate example of sacrifice. Jesus said that we have a cross (a sacrifice) to take up so that we can follow Him. *"And he who does not take his cross and follow after Me is not worthy of Me" (Matthew 10:38–39).* Jesus says that if we refuse our cross (our sacrificial life), we are not worthy of Him. He wants us to know that His cross (sacrifice) was on *our* behalf and that our cross (sacrifice) is on *His* behalf.

God Rewards Sacrifice

God notices our sacrifices and generously rewards us for them—now, and in eternity as Mark 10:29–30 says:

> *Assuredly, I say to you, there is no one who has left house or brothers or sisters or father or mother or wife or children or lands, for My sake and the gospel's, who shall not receive a hundredfold now in this time—houses and brothers and sisters and mothers and children and lands, with persecutions—and in the age to come, eternal life.*

God Loves Joyful Sacrifice

God loves it when we sacrifice material things cheerfully—not reluctantly or under compulsion. He wants us to give from what is in our hearts so that we can give joyfully. *"Each man should give what he has decided in his heart to give, not reluctantly or under compulsion, for God loves a cheerful giver" (2 Corinthians 9:7 NIV).*

The amount of the sacrifice it takes to give determines the value of the gift. In other words, the more it costs us to give, the more valuable it is to God and others. We see this fact when Jesus watched how people put money into the treasury—He watched the rich put in much and a poor widow put in her two cents:

> *One poor widow came up and put in two small coins—a measly two cents. Jesus called his disciples over and said, "The truth is that this poor widow gave more to the collection than all the others put together. All the others gave what they'll never miss; she gave extravagantly what she couldn't afford—she gave her all." (Mark 12:42–44 TMSG)*

It's not what we give, but how we give that is most important; therefore, we have a right to give sacrificially.

A Continual Sacrifice

God desires the continual sacrifice of praise, not just "an hour on Sunday."

> *Therefore by Him let us continually offer the sacrifice of praise to God, that is, the fruit of our lips, giving thanks to His name. But do not forget to do good and to share, for with such sacrifices God is well pleased. (Hebrews 13:15–16)*

Notice that the words "with such sacrifices" are in the plural. God loves our sacrifice of praise, but He also expects our sacrifice of sharing and doing good for these *two* sacrifices (praising and doing) bring God great pleasure.

Let's live the sacrificial life we have the right to live in Christ.

The Right to Know and Do God's Will

The Importance of Scripture

To do the will of God, we must first know the will of God. There are two main ways to know the will of God—the Bible and the Holy Spirit. We will first consider the Bible.

Our emphasis should be on the Bible because it shows us God's will. Thus, we can know God's will for many areas of our lives by simply knowing what the Bible teaches. It's also great to know and believe what a pastor or teacher says about the Bible, but we should still be like the people in Acts 17:11:

> . . . *They were very willing to receive God's message, and every day they carefully examined the Scriptures to see if what Paul said was true. (GW)*

To sum up what we are saying: We should not just receive the word of men without knowing that the Scriptures support it. This does not mean that we need to be a theologian, but we should all be familiar with the Bible's teachings.

The Importance of the Holy Spirit

The next primary way to know the will of God is by the Holy Spirit. The Father sent the Holy Spirit to live within us so that we can know His will. Jesus said that the Holy

Spirit would be our teacher and would help us remember what He, Jesus, taught us.

> *But the Helper, the Holy Spirit, whom the Father will send in My name, He will teach you all things, and bring to your remembrance all things that I said to you. (John 14:26)*

If we follow the leading of the Holy Spirit, we will be doing the will of God rather than giving place to sinful actions (things contrary to the will of God). *"So I say, live by the Spirit, and you will not gratify the desires of the sinful nature"* (Galatians 5:16 NIV).

In addition, the Holy Spirit produces the outgrowth (fruit) of God's Spirit in our lives:

> *But the fruit of the Spirit is love, joy, peace, patience, kindness, goodness, faithfulness, gentleness and self-control . . . (Galatians 5:22–23 NIV)*

Also, the Holy Spirit helps us to pray according to the will of God when we do not know His will.

> *Now He who searches the hearts knows what the mind of the Spirit is, because He makes intercession for the saints according to the will of God. (Romans 8:27)*

It Is Not Enough to Just Know His Will

After we have the knowledge of God's will, we need to do His will. *"Do what God's word says. Don't merely listen to it . . ."* (James 1:22 GW).

Jesus asks us a serious question in Luke 6:46, *"But why do you call Me 'Lord, Lord,' and not do the things which I say?"*

Furthermore, Jesus says that His sheep know His voice (know His will) and that they follow Him (do His will). *"My sheep hear My voice, and I know them, and they follow Me" (John 10:27).*

We have the right to know His will and to do His will, which is how we are fulfilled as Christians—by knowing *and* doing His will.

Knowing God

We know who God is by the Scriptures and by the Holy Spirit. Additionally, we can know God by just being in His presence; that is, sometimes we know the will of God simply because we *know* Him—to know Jesus personally is the best way to know what God the Father is like. When we see who Jesus is, then we see who the Father is. *"He who has seen Me has seen the Father . . ." (John 14:9).*

To sum up what we are saying, knowing God personally through the Bible, the Holy Spirit, and His presence, is the best way to know His will. Then when we know His will, we can do His will, which is our Christian right.

Day 14

The Right to Love Our Enemies

Our Beliefs

As you have noticed, I have used an abundance of Scripture in each chapter so that we can have our beliefs based upon the Bible—we believe what we believe because it is the Word of God. And because of those beliefs, we will have enemies. Jesus said in John 15:20, *"If they persecuted Me, they will also persecute you."*

Guaranteed Persecution

Jesus said in the above verse, *"If they persecuted Me, they will also persecute you."* So if they persecuted Jesus, that guarantees our persecution. We all know that Jesus was persecuted in many ways, even unto death; therefore, we are *guaranteed* enemies that will persecute us—if we are a true Christian.

Loving Our Enemies

As a Christian, we have the right to love those who persecute us; Jesus Himself gave us this right. However, if we do not understand the power of this right, then we will think we do not need it or want it.

So why would we want to love our enemies? The reason for loving our enemies is so that we can be like the Father in heaven and His Son Jesus Christ. They are the examples given for us to follow. Even so, we may not have followed their examples very often or at all.

Jesus not only *showed* us how to treat our enemies by example, He also *taught* us how in Matthew 5:43–45:

> *You have heard that it was said, "You shall love your neighbor and hate your enemy." But I say to you, love your enemies, bless those who curse you, do good to those who hate you, and pray for those who spitefully use you and persecute you . . .*

Overcome Evil with Good

The Father in heaven knows the best way to respond to our enemies; He says to overcome evil with good. We all know this is not the usual human response to evil. The normal human response seems to be to repay evil for evil. However, the response we are to have as Christians is in Romans 12:20–21:

> *. . . If your enemy is hungry, feed him; if he is thirsty, give him something to drink. . . . Do not be overcome by evil, but overcome evil with good. (NIV)*

Being Merciful to Our Enemies

Jesus wants us to love our enemies and to be merciful to them. Why does He want us to be merciful to our enemies? Jesus says the reason is so that we can be like our Heavenly Father—He is merciful. Jesus shows us this in Luke 6:35–36:

> *Rather, love your enemies, do good to them, and lend to them, expecting nothing in return. Then your reward will be great, and you will*

be children of the Most High, for he is kind to
ungrateful and evil people. Be merciful, just as
your Father is merciful. (ISV)

If we love our enemies as Jesus taught us to love them, our reward will be great and *"you will be children of the Most High."* We, as God's children, are to reflect Him to everyone, including our enemies. By being merciful to our enemies, we reflect the love and mercy God has for them. Furthermore, we may see our enemies saved from their sin when we reflect God to them. Indeed, that would be a great reward—seeing an enemy become a child of God.

God is so merciful that He can forgive even His greatest enemies—like the Apostle Paul. Remember, Saul (Paul) was one of God's greatest enemies, but God showed him mercy (see 1 Timothy 1:15–16 and Acts 9).

Day 15

The Right to Work

Work

We usually think of work as labor, toil, effort, and exertion. However, we have all noticed that if we *love* doing something, it does not seem like work at all. Could it be that our attitude concerning work is as important as the work itself? Yes, because what we think about our work determines whether we think it is work we *have to* do, or work we *get to* do. Just like loving the work lightens it, so hating the work increases it. Therefore, work can be enjoyable or unbearable, based upon our attitude regarding the work.

An excellent example of this is found in the story of Jacob working for Laban to obtain Rachel for his wife:

> *So Jacob served seven years for Rachel, and they seemed only a few days to him because of the love he had for her. (Genesis 29:20)*

Another example is the attitude of those who worked in Exodus 36:2; they worked because it was in their hearts to work—". . . *whose heart was stirred, to come and do the work.*" Another Bible translation of this verse says, ". . . *The men were eager to get started and engage in the work*" (TMSG).

Work from Our Hearts

As stated previously, the men in Exodus 36 were so eager to work because it was in their hearts to do the work. But how did they have the desire in their hearts to do the work? The answer is: God's giftings enable us to have it in our hearts to do the work—*". . . every skilled person to whom the LORD has given skill and ability to know how to carry out all the work . . ." (Exodus 36:1 NIV).* Accordingly, we all have gifts from God to do a specific work; for that reason, our work can come from our hearts. Thus, we can enjoy the work we do if it is what God has gifted us to do.

I have been discussing the actual physical work we do; now, I will look at the *work of God* that He calls us into.

The Work of God

Most of us have desired to do the work of God. But what is the work of God? Jesus was asked this question in John 6:28–29:

> *Then they said to Him, "What shall we do, that we may work the works of God?" Jesus answered and said to them, "This is the work of God, that you believe in Him whom He sent." (John 6:28–29)*

We need to understand Jesus' answer to their question. His answer means that the work of God is to get us to come to Jesus and to believe in Him (Jesus). However, the Scriptures show us that no one can come to Jesus without God drawing him or her—teaching us to totally trust in Jesus. In John 6:44–45, Jesus explains this:

> *No one can come to me unless the Father who sent me draws him, and I will raise him to life on the last day. It is written in the Prophets,*

"And all of them will be taught by God."
Everyone who has listened to the Father and
has learned anything comes to me. (ISV)

God is working in our lives to get us to believe all He says about His Son—changing us from trusting in ourselves to trusting in His Son Jesus. His work includes getting us to believe things such as Philippians 4:13, *"I can do all things through Christ who strengthens me."* And Philippians 4:19, *"And my God shall supply all your need according to His riches in glory by Christ Jesus."* And 2 Corinthians 5:17, *"Therefore, if anyone is in Christ, he is a new creation; old things have passed away; behold, all things have become new."*

Notice in these verses that it is *through Christ, by Christ,* and *in Christ* that these things happen—because everything God does is through Jesus. Thus, the work of God is exalting Jesus to a place of preeminence (first place) in our lives.

In summary, the work of God causes us to believe wholly in Jesus, which means that we do not trust in ourselves, we trust in Jesus—knowing that we will never be adequate to do the work of God by ourselves. Our ability to do any work, whether physical or spiritual, comes from God. We should never think that we are adequate in ourselves.

> *Not that we are sufficient of ourselves to think*
> *of anything as being from ourselves, but our*
> *sufficiency is from God. (2 Corinthians 3:5)*

The Apostle Paul did not think he was adequate in himself, he knew his sufficiency was from God and that

God could enable him to be abundantly sufficient for every good work (see 2 Corinthians 9:8).

God's work causes us to trust totally in Jesus—to believe completely in Jesus for everything and in every situation. We have the right to enter into the work of God—to know and believe Jesus completely!

The Right to Prosper and Be in Health

John's Desire

"The Elder [John], to the beloved Gaius, whom I love in truth: beloved, I pray that you may prosper in all things and be in health, just as your soul prospers" (3 John 1:1–2). The Apostle John desired for Gaius to prosper and be in health. Do we have the same desire of wanting the very best for others? Or, have we been jealous of another's prosperity or health because our health or prosperity was not as great? If so, do we realize that our judgment of another's prosperity or health could be the reason we are not prospering or experiencing health? *"That critical spirit has a way of boomeranging" (Matthew 7:2 TMSG).*

God's Desire

We have the right to believe God wants the very best for us, because His apostles speak for Him, especially when it is inspired Scripture. So then, John is speaking for God when he says, *"Beloved, I pray that you may prosper in all things and be in health, just as your soul prospers" (3 John 1:2).*

First, we see that the words "just as" show us that God desires the very best for us in earthly things *and* spiritual things. That is, God wants us to believe for more equality between heaven and earth. In heaven there is only prosperity and health and He wants the heavenly to come to the earth. Jesus taught us to pray, *"Your kingdom* come. *Your will be done on earth as it is in heaven"* (*Matthew 6:10).* So when we pray "the Lord's Prayer" we are actually praying for our prosperity in all things including our health. In other words, we have the right to prosper and be in health since Jesus taught us to pray for the heavenly to come upon the earth.

Second, we see that the words "just as" show us that God wants us to prosper and be healthy even as He desires our souls' prosperity. Our souls prosper by us walking in the *truth,* and when our soul is prospering, prosperity and health flow easily to us.

Walking in Truth

Again, one of the greatest hindrances to our health and prosperity is our criticism of others. Criticizing others is not walking in the truth; it is disobedience to the truth. Disobedience can hinder our prosperity and health because God's promises are conditional. Notice in the following verses that God promises us health and prosperity **if** we quit pointing our fingers and criticizing others; moreover, instead of criticizing others, God expects us to help others:

> . . . *Your healing shall spring forth speedily . . .*
> *If you take away the yoke from your midst,*
> *The pointing of the finger, and speaking wickedness,*
>
> *If you extend your soul to the hungry*
> *And satisfy the afflicted soul . . .*
> *You shall be like a watered garden,*
> *And like a spring of water, whose waters do not fail. (Isaiah 58:8–11)*

These verses show that prosperity and health are conditional upon our walking in truth, which includes not criticizing others.

Another part of walking in truth is realizing that God wants us to trust in Him for our health and prosperity instead of our own abilities. Therefore, we should not be boasting about how *we* are going to do this or that, or how *we* are going to prosper as James 4:13–16 states:

> *Now listen, you who say, "Today or tomorrow we will go to this or that city, spend a year there, carry on business and make money."* . . . *Instead, you ought to say, "If it is the Lord's will, we will live and do this or that." As it is, you boast and brag. All such boasting is evil.* (NIV)

We will see another key issue to our prosperity in the next chapter.

Day 17

The Right to Assemble

What it Does Not Mean

One of the primary Scriptures used to show that we have a right to assemble is Hebrews 10:25:

> . . . *not forsaking the assembling of ourselves together, as is the manner of some, but exhorting one another, and so much the more as you see the Day approaching.*

This Scripture has been misinterpreted many times to have the *one and only* meaning that we should regularly attend church. However, *"not forsaking the assembling of ourselves together,"* means more than just going to church every time the doors are open. Certainly, it includes "going to church" for that is a good place to begin to assemble. Nonetheless, we must go beyond simply thinking of the assembling of Christians together as just attending church.

What it Does Mean

What does it mean for Christians to have the right to assemble? The Greek word carries the idea of a complete collection, the assembling (gathering) together of believers. The English word *assemble* means: "fitting parts of something together" or "to put different components together."

We see from the meaning of the word *assemble* that it means more than simply attending church services, since you can attend church services and still never be joined with other believers. To have the right to assemble means that we have the right of "joining to" the rest of the body of Christ.

In 1 Corinthians 12, Paul speaks of what it means to be assembled together. He shows us that we are the body of Christ and that all the body parts must be joined (assembled) together just like in the human body to function properly. For what use is a part of the body that is not functioning properly? Or what use is a part of the body that is separated from it? The only way a part of the body has any meaning or usefulness is if it is assembled (joined) to the body. "*. . . Only as you accept your part of that body does your 'part' mean anything"* (1 Corinthians 12:27 TMSG).

Am I saying that we do not need to "go to church" regularly? No, for how can we be a part of the body if we do not come together with it? I am saying that "going to church" is but a *beginning* step of being assembled together. Why? Because it is all about having a living relationship with other believers, which means we will have to be with other believers on a regular basis. This can include larger church gatherings as well as smaller home gatherings, in addition to living life together with other believers throughout the week.

Why Assemble?

First, our meeting together is for motivating each other, which is something *every* Christian needs— encouragement to love and do good deeds. And in the days we are living in, we need even more encouragement as Hebrews 10:24–25 states:

And let us continue to consider how to stimulate one another to love and good deeds, not neglecting to meet together, as is the habit of some, but encouraging one another even more as you see the day coming nearer. (ISV)

Second, and perhaps most important, it truly pleases God when we assemble in harmony, which is the very atmosphere of heaven—perfect unity with God and with others. Even so, the heart of God is for us to be one with Him and with one another while still on this earth. This is evident as we see Jesus' heart when He prayed, *"May they be brought to complete unity to let the world know that you sent me and have loved them even as you have loved me" (John 17:23 NIV).*

John chapter 17 shows us several times that God wants us to be one with one another *just as* Father God is one with His Son Jesus Christ.

God says our unity with one another is good and pleasant, *"See how good and pleasant it is when brothers and sisters live together in harmony!" (Psalm 133:1 GW).* Then in verse 3 we see that there is something eternal we touch when we live together with other believers in harmony:

That is where the LORD promised the blessing of eternal life. (Psalm 133:3 GW)

Day 18

The Right to Trust God

What Is Trust?

Trust is a powerful word that signifies a relationship with something or someone. In this chapter, I will use the word *trust* as it relates to God. And because we have a relationship with God, we can trust Him; and the greater our relationship with Him, the greater our trust in Him can be.

To trust God means: to be confident in Him, to be sure of Him, to hope in Him, to flee to Him for protection, security and refuge. It is: having faith in Him, relying on Him, depending on Him, and counting on Him. In other words, it is trusting in *HIM;* that is, we are trusting in His very nature—in all He is. Therefore, the more we truly know Him, the more we will truly trust Him.

It Takes Humility

At times, we can find ourselves trusting in our own ideas, thoughts, and opinions instead of acknowledging God and His opinion—including even the important choices in our lives. Our pride thinks we do not need God's viewpoint.

The fact is, it takes humility to trust what God says about a matter instead of what we think. We need to trust God in all of our ways and not lean on our own ideas, letting God direct us.

Trust in the Lord with all your heart,
And lean not on your own understanding;

In all your ways acknowledge Him,
And He shall direct your paths.
Do not be wise in your own eyes . . .
(Proverbs 3:5–7)

Our trust in God enables us to humble ourselves by casting *all* our cares, worries, and anxieties upon Him— knowing that He really cares for us. If we do not cast *all* of our cares upon Him, it is because we do not *totally* trust that He cares for us. However as our trust in Him grows, we will cast more and more of our cares upon Him; and as we humble ourselves in this way, we can then expect a greater measure of His grace.

"*God resists the proud, But gives grace to the humble.*"

Therefore humble yourselves under the mighty hand of God . . . casting all your care upon Him, for He cares for you. (1 Peter 5:5–7)

Trusting God with Our Possessions

Trusting God can deliver us from the root of all evil. That is to say, God gives us ways to trust Him with our possessions that will help break the power of the love of money—the root of all evil.

If we want to increase in material possessions, we should first make sure we are following God's principles about material things, which will keep the root of evil from afflicting us. If the love of money has already taken root in us, God's Biblical principles can deliver us. Some of these principles are in 1 Timothy 6:9–11:

But they that will be rich fall into temptation and a snare, and into many foolish and hurtful lusts, which drown men in destruction and perdition. For the love of money is the root of all evil: which while some coveted after, they have erred from the faith, and pierced themselves through with many sorrows. But thou, O man of God, flee these things; and follow after righteousness, godliness, faith, love, patience, meekness. (KJV)

God's directions on how to use our possessions will deliver us from the love of money. Additionally, if we will trust God and use our possessions His way, He will be able to trust us with His abundant blessings.

Can a person cheat God? Yet, you are cheating me! But you ask, "How are we cheating you?" When you don't bring a tenth of your income and other contributions. So a curse is on you because the whole nation is cheating me! Bring one-tenth of your income into the storehouse so that there may be food in my house. Test me in this way, says the LORD of Armies. See if I won't open the windows of heaven for you and flood you with blessings. (Malachi 3:8–10 GW)

God knows that the giving away of a portion of our possessions will help keep our hearts free from the love of money. Then as we give from our hearts, God will give us His rich blessings as 2 Corinthians 9:7–8 states:

So let each one give as he purposes in his heart, not grudgingly or of necessity; for God loves a cheerful giver. And God is able to make all grace abound toward you, that you, always having all sufficiency in all things, may have an abundance for every good work.

How we deal with our finances may be God's test to see if He can trust us with the true riches of His kingdom:

Whoever can be trusted with very little can also be trusted with much, and whoever is dishonest with very little will also be dishonest with much. So if you have not been trustworthy in handling worldly wealth, who will trust you with true riches? (Luke 16:10–11 NIV)

Peace in Trusting God

When we trust someone, we can be at peace in any situation concerning him or her. When we trust God, we will be in perfect peace in every situation. *"You will keep him in perfect peace, Whose mind is stayed on You, Because he trusts in You"* (Isaiah 26:3).

In the next chapter, we will see what God calls a person who trusts in Him and does what He says.

The Right to Be a Friend of God

What Is a Friend?

Friendship is not just something that happens; friendship requires a certain amount of familiarity, closeness, and companionship. The Bible says that to have friends we must be friendly (see Proverbs 18:24). To say it another way, to be a friend we have to be open to the closeness, familiarity, and companionship of another person; then because of the time spent together, we create an emotional connection with that person. Therefore, a friend is someone who is willing to be emotionally close to another person, to be fond of them, and to trust them.

Friendship with God

If we want to be a friend of God, it requires our faith. Faith in God opens the door to friendship with Him; then when the door to friendship with God is open, faith works to make sure the friendship is established. We see this in the life of Abraham in James 2:22–23:

> *You see that his faith was active with his works, and by his works faith was made complete. And so the Scripture was fulfilled that says, "Abraham believed God, and it was credited to him as righteousness." So he was called God's friend. (ISV)*

The Scriptures show that Abraham is the father of faith *and* the friend of God because the two go together.

Remember friendship requires an emotional investment, and Abraham had a very emotional investment with God—he was required to offer his son Isaac. So when he offered this great emotional investment, the son he greatly loved, God received Abraham's faith and called him His friend.

What emotional thing in your life is God testing you with to see if you will offer it up to Him? God trusts you enough to test you in order that you may be His friend. So let's trust Him with everything in our lives—because friends trust each other.

Jesus' Friends

If we want to be Jesus' friend, we simply must do whatever He commands. He commands us to love one another just as He loved us. In other words, we cannot be Jesus' friend if we do not love one another.

> *This is My commandment, that you love one another as I have loved you. Greater love has no one than this, than to lay down one's life for his friends. You are My friends if you do whatever I command you. (John 15:12–14)*

Jesus calls us *friends* when we do whatever He commands us from a heart of love.

Wrong Friendship

Is there a friendship that will make us an enemy of God? Yes! Therefore, no matter what the cost, we should avoid that friendship. What is the friendship that will make us God's enemy? We find the answer to this question in James 4:4–5:

You adulterers! Don't you know that friendship with the world means hostility with God? So whoever wants to be a friend of this world is an enemy of God. Or do you think the Scripture means nothing when it says that the Spirit that God caused to live in us jealously yearns for us? (ISV)

God calls friendship with the world adultery. Why is this true? It is true because the Holy Spirit that lives in us jealously yearns for us. Consequently, God does not want the world to be our friend; He wants to be our friend! That is why He calls it adultery when we choose friendship with the world over friendship with Him. In fact, He says that if are a friend with the world, we are an enemy of God. So let's choose God, come close to Him, and be His friend.

The Right to Be Disciplined

What is Discipline?

Discipline is bringing order and control to our lives by training and correction. This instruction can come in the form of teaching, or in the form of a rebuke or reproof. At times, discipline may come in the form of punishment—not for the purpose of punishment, but for the purpose of training, correction, and teaching—to educate us to live right.

It Is Not Strange

We should never think of the Lord's discipline as strange or unusual whether it is happening to us or to someone else. The only thing we should think of as unusual is being without discipline. Why is that? It's because He loves us, which means He will correct us when we need it. Hebrews 12:8 says that if a person is without discipline, then that person is not God's child, *"If you are not disciplined (and everyone undergoes discipline), then you are illegitimate children and not true sons." (NIV)*

Discipline by the Word

One major way our parents disciplined us was by their words. God also disciplines us through His Word:

> *All Scripture is given by inspiration of God, and is profitable for doctrine, for reproof, for correction, for instruction in righteousness . . . (2 Timothy 3:16–17)*

This would be a good time to ask ourselves some questions. Have we avoided certain passages in the Bible because we do not want the discipline those passages would give us? Or, have we gone beyond that and refrained from reading the Bible because we do not want it confronting something in our life?

God gave us the Bible for our benefit; therefore, we have the right to desire its discipline. The Bible is our Heavenly Father's word to us and He disciplines us by it so we will live better lives now, and in eternity. Let's pay attention to His discipline since it is for our good. We may not enjoy His discipline while it is happening; but in the end, we will rejoice over every time He disciplined us if we see that it was for our good. Knowing this, we may even be bold as King David in Psalm 139:23–24 and say:

> *Search me, O God, and know my heart;*
> *Try me, and know my anxieties;*
> *And see if there is any wicked way in me,*
> *And lead me in the way everlasting.*

The Book of Proverbs

The book of Proverbs has much to say about discipline and the wisdom in submitting to it; therefore, we will quote a few of the passages from this important book on discipline.

> *But don't, dear friend, resent God's discipline;*
> * don't sulk under his loving correction.*
> *It's the child he loves that God corrects;*
> * a father's delight is behind all this.*
> *(Proverbs 3:11–12 TMSG)*

Oh, how I hated discipline!
How my heart despised correction!
I didn't listen to what my teachers said to me,
    nor did I keep my ear open to my instructors.
I almost reached total ruin in the assembly
    and in the congregation.
(Proverbs 5:12–14 GW)

Whoever loves discipline loves knowledge,
    but he who hates correction is stupid.
(Proverbs 12:1 NIV)

Poverty and shame come to a person who
        ignores discipline,
    but whoever pays attention to constructive
        criticism will be honored.
(Proverbs 13:18 GW)

Do not hesitate to discipline a child.
If you spank him, he will not die.
Spank him yourself, and you will save his soul
        from hell.
(Proverbs 23:13–14 GW)

A spanking and a warning produce wisdom,
    but an undisciplined child disgraces his
        mother.
(Proverbs 29:15 GW)

Discipline your children; you'll be glad you did—
    they'll turn out delightful to live with.
(Proverbs 29:17 TMSG)

God in His wisdom disciplines us so that we can live disciplined lives—being a blessing to Him and to the world. Therefore, we should gladly embrace our right to be disciplined by God. Also, He expects us to discipline our children in wisdom so that they will live disciplined lives—to be a blessing to society.

Day 21

The Right to Be Free from Anger

The Fruit of Anger

There are two kinds of anger: *righteous anger* and *unrighteous anger*. Righteous anger produces righteous fruit—fruit God calls good. Unrighteous anger produces unrighteous fruit—fruit God calls bad. Thus, anger can be good or bad depending upon the fruit that it produces.

Jesus was angry with the religious leaders in Mark 3:5 when they did not want Him to heal on the Sabbath; nevertheless, He still healed a man that needed healing even though He was angry. He produced good fruit in His anger.

We see that God gets angry in Psalm 30:5, but only for a moment:

> *For His anger is but for a moment,*
> *His favor is for life . . .*

Since God gets angry, He does not forbid us from getting angry; however, He warns us not to sin when we are angry and to get rid of our anger quickly lest we give an opportunity to the devil. *"Be angry, and do not sin": do not let the sun go down on your wrath, nor give place to the devil" (Ephesians 4:26).*

The Seriousness of Anger

Anger can be the first sign of the possibility of murder! In other words, *murder* can take root in our hearts when we are angry with someone, especially if we refuse to get over it. Also, being angry with someone can result in name-calling, which Jesus says is a very serious matter:

> *You have heard that it was said to those of old, "You shall not murder, and whoever murders will be in danger of the judgment." But I say to you that whoever is angry with his brother without a cause shall be in danger of the judgment. And whoever says to his brother, "Raca!" shall be in danger of the council. But whoever says, "You fool!" shall be in danger of hell fire. (Matthew 5:21–22)*

The anger that we can be free from is *unrighteous anger*. Unrighteous anger produces the bad fruit of "name-calling," and at times, murder.

What Is Murder?

The word *murder* means: to smite with deadly intent, to put to death, to slay, to slaughter, to dash in pieces—to kill a human being. Murder is the taking of the life of another person deliberately, not in self-defense. Murder is a serious sin that has very serious consequences.

In addition to this, the Scriptures expand the definition of murder to hating a brother or sister in Christ. *"Everyone who hates another believer is a murderer, and you know that a murderer doesn't have eternal life"* (1 John 3:15 GW).

Can We Find Murderers in Scripture?

The first sin recorded in the Bible after Adam and Eve's sin was murder—Cain murdered Abel.

*Not as Cain who was of the wicked one and
murdered his brother. And why did he murder
him? Because his works were evil and his
brother's righteous. (1 John 3:12)*

Also, we see that some of the greatest heroes of the
Bible were guilty of murder: Moses murdered a man (see
Exodus 2:11–12); King David murdered a man (see
2 Samuel 12); and the Apostle Paul bore some
responsibility for murder (see Acts 7:58–8:3). From these
examples, we see that *anyone* can be capable of murder—
especially when we consider God's definition of a
murderer as anyone who hates a brother or sister in
Christ.

Is Murder Forgivable?

As stated earlier, murder is a serious sin that has very
serious consequences, but it is forgivable. Jesus said *all*
sin is forgivable except blasphemy of the Holy Spirit.

*Wherefore I say unto you, All manner of sin
and blasphemy shall be forgiven unto men: but
the blasphemy against the Holy Ghost shall not
be forgiven unto men. (Matthew 12:31 KJV)*

Currently, some do not realize that abortion is a form
of murder. Abortion is the shedding of innocent blood (an
unborn child is innocent blood). Proverbs 6:16–17
declares:

*These six things the LORD hates,
Yes, seven are an abomination to Him:
A proud look,*

A lying tongue,
Hands that shed innocent blood . . .

If we have been involved with abortion in any way, it is essential to know that we can be forgiven. How can we be forgiven? The Bible gives us the simple answer; it is found in Jesus and our faith in Him. To be forgiven, we must simply acknowledge the fact that the abortion was sin and confess the sin to God; then He is faithful to forgive. Furthermore, God says that He is *just* to forgive us of this sin and to cleanse us from it.

> *If we confess our sins, He is faithful and just to forgive us our sins and to cleanse us from all unrighteousness. If we say that we have not sinned, we make Him a liar, and His word is not in us. (1 John 1:9–10)*

Praying the prayer that King David prayed after he was guilty of murder can help anyone guilty of murder.

> *Rescue me from the guilt of murder,*
> *O God, my savior . . .*
> *You are not happy with any sacrifice.*
> *Otherwise, I would offer one to you . . .*
> *The sacrifice pleasing to God is a broken spirit.*
> *O God, you do not despise a broken and*
> *   sorrowful heart.*
> *(Psalm 51:14–17 GW)*

Sowing and Reaping

Even though we can be totally forgiven and free from the sin of murder, it does not mean that murder does not have serious consequences. Murderers may spend years in prison or be put to death. That does not mean that God did not forgive them if they repented and confessed their sin; it simply means that a person reaps what he sows. *"Do not be deceived, God is not mocked; for whatever a man sows, that he will also reap" (Galatians 6:7).*

Reaping what we have sown does not mean that we have to live with shame and guilt. When God forgives us, shame and guilt should no longer be a part of our lives, although we may have to live with the consequences of the sin. As we know, murder has serious consequences but so does God's forgiveness! Without a doubt, we should allow God's forgiveness to have more power in our lives than any sin or its consequences.

Day 22

The Right to Have Passion

What is Passion?

Passion is a strong desire, liking, or enthusiasm for something; it is an intense emotion. And when we speak of passion with a capital "P" as in the *Passion of Christ,* it speaks of the sufferings of Jesus Christ from the Last Supper until His crucifixion—because there has never been a greater passion expressed than when Jesus suffered and died for us. In other words, passion is not just having intense emotions; it is the acting out of those emotions. In the example of Jesus, His inward passion was the tremendous love for His Father and for us; then, He expressed that passion outwardly in His sufferings and death.

Passion is something that starts within and then expresses itself outwardly. A person who is passionate for something cannot hide it for long, for others will see it expressed outwardly.

Examples of Passion

There are degrees of passion. The ultimate examples and possessors of passion are God the Father, His Son Jesus Christ, and the Holy Spirit. First, their passion is unmatched *inwardly*—for the greatest passion is love, and God *is* love. Second, their passion is unmatched *outwardly* because no one ever showed the degree of love that God did through His Son Jesus Christ.

Also, humans can have a high degree of passion since God created men and women in His image. Here are some examples of humanity's passion:

> Enoch walked with God for three hundred years! Noah spent many years building an ark to save the animals and humanity. Abraham did not withhold his own son but offered him to God. Moses wanted above all things to know God, to have His presence with him and to see His glory. Hannah, who was barren, cried out to God for a male child; then gave him up to the Lord's work. Mary, who was a virgin, allowed God to impregnate her because she loved God more than her reputation.

Then we have King David, a man after God's own heart, who expressed great passion for God in Psalm 27:

> *One thing I have desired of the LORD,*
> *That will I seek:*
> *That I may dwell in the house of the LORD*
> *All the days of my life,*
> *To behold the beauty of the LORD,*
> *And to inquire in His temple. (verse 4)*

> *When You said, "Seek My face,"*
> *My heart said to You, "Your face, LORD,*
> *I will seek." (verse 8)*

Then we have the sons of Korah expressing their passion for God in Psalm 42:1–2:

> *As the deer pants for the water brooks,*
> *So pants my soul for You, O God.*

My soul thirsts for God, for the living God.
When shall I come and appear before God?

The Book of Passion

Probably the most common way we hear passion expressed is in song—songs of passion. When we think of worship, we usually think of songs sung unto the Lord since there is something about a song that expresses our passion as few other things can. Because when we are singing with the music, it becomes easier to release our passion for the Lord.

God knows how that passion and song go together, so He gave us a complete book of the Bible on passion that is actually a song. It's called "Song of Solomon" in some Bibles and "Song of Songs" in others. It starts out with the phrase "the song of songs" which could have been translated as "highest song" or "best song of all" as we see in one translation: *"The song—best of all songs—Solomon's song!" (Song of Songs 1:1 TMSG).*

This song is the best of all the songs that Solomon wrote because of how well it speaks of God's passion for us and our passion for Him. In other words, the whole book of the Song of Solomon is all about passion; the following verses are just a few examples of this:

> *Take me away with you! Let's run off together!*
> *An elopement with my King–Lover!*
> *We'll celebrate, we'll sing, we'll make great*
>   *music.*
> *Yes! For your love is better than vintage wine.*
> *(Song of Songs 1:4 TMSG)*

He brought me to the banqueting house,
And his banner over me was love.
Sustain me with cakes of raisins,
Refresh me with apples,
For I am lovesick.
(Song of Solomon 2:4–5)

You have ravished my heart,
My sister, my spouse;
You have ravished my heart
With one look of your eyes,
With one link of your necklace.
(Song of Solomon 4:9)

Many waters cannot quench love,
Nor can the floods drown it.
If a man would give for love
All the wealth of his house,
It would be utterly despised.
(Song of Solomon 8:7)

We can see from these Scriptures that God is very passionate and that He gives us the right to be passionate; therefore, do not let anyone quench your passion but let God fan your passion into the blaze He desires!

The Right to the Supernatural

What Is the Supernatural?

The supernatural is that which is "super-natural"—that which is beyond the natural. First, as it relates to us as Christians, it is the power of the Holy Spirit working in and through us. This power of the Holy Spirit often manifests through us in the gifts of the Spirit and God does not want us to be ignorant of these gifts. *"Now about spiritual gifts, brothers, I do not want you to be ignorant" (1 Corinthians 12:1 NIV).*

Some of the supernatural gifts from the Holy Spirit are listed in 1 Corinthians 12:8–10:

> *To one there is given through the Spirit the message of wisdom, to another the message of knowledge by means of the same Spirit, to another faith by the same Spirit, to another gifts of healing by that one Spirit, to another miraculous powers, to another prophecy, to another distinguishing between spirits, to another speaking in different kinds of tongues, to still another the interpretation of tongues. (NIV)*

Not all of the gifts of the Spirit seem to be supernatural even though they are gifts from God since they can seem quite extraordinary, or at other times, quite natural. That is, prophecy (speaking under the inspiration of the Spirit) appears supernatural, while serving, teaching, encouraging, leading, or showing mercy seem quite natural even though these are also gifts from God as Romans 12:6–8 says:

> *We have different gifts, according to the grace given us. If a man's gift is prophesying, let him use it in proportion to his faith. If it is serving, let him serve; if it is teaching, let him teach; if it is encouraging, let him encourage; if it is contributing to the needs of others, let him give generously; if it is leadership, let him govern diligently; if it is showing mercy, let him do it cheerfully (NIV).*

Second, the supernatural is the spiritual realm. God and His created beings inhabit this realm and can interact with us. Of course, this is also the realm of the devil and his fallen angels.

We see many examples of interacting with the spiritual realm in the Scriptures. As we know, Jesus constantly interacted with the spiritual realm—especially in prayer. Indeed, prayer is a most common way we interact with the spiritual realm.

Also, Jesus set the example of interacting with the spiritual realm by supernaturally healing the sick, cleansing the lepers, raising the dead, and casting demons out, and He commanded us to do the same. *"Heal the sick, cleanse the lepers, raise the dead, cast out demons. Freely you have received, freely give" (Matthew 10:8).*

Additionally, Jesus said that supernatural signs would follow those who believe in Him as Mark 16:17–18 states:

*And these signs will follow those who believe:
In My name they will cast out demons; they
will speak with new tongues; they will take up
serpents; and if they drink anything deadly, it
will by no means hurt them; they will lay
hands on the sick, and they will recover.*

The Supernatural Book

The Bible is a supernatural book. First, because God breathed it out—it is the very words of God. *"All Scripture is God-breathed . . ." (2 Timothy 3:16 ISV).*

Second, the Bible is a supernatural book because it is a book about God's interaction with man; it is God's history book (*His*-story book). And throughout the Old and New Testaments, we find God's supernatural works.

Third, the Bible is a supernatural book because it shows *men and women* doing supernatural exploits by their faith in God. In Hebrews chapter 11 we observe many supernatural things that men and women accomplished by their faith in God; like having children when their bodies were too old to conceive; or people passing through the Red Sea as on dry land; or having the walls of Jericho fall flat with their shout. We even see that women received their dead raised to life again!

Then there are many other supernatural things recorded throughout the rest of the Bible that men and women accomplished through their faith in God.

The Right to the Supernatural

We have the right to the supernatural because:

1. God is supernatural and He created us in His image.

2. Jesus is supernatural and we are to abide in Him.
3. The Holy Spirit is supernatural and we are His temple.
4. The Bible is supernatural and we are to live by its teachings.
5. The Church is supernaturally built by Jesus of which we are a part.
6. The Holy Spirit is poured out on all in the last days:

> *In the last days, God says, I will pour my Spirit on everyone. Your sons and daughters will speak what God has revealed. Your young men will see visions. Your old men will dream dreams. In those days I will pour my Spirit on my servants, on both men and women. They will speak what God has revealed. I will work miracles in the sky and give signs on the earth: blood, fire, and clouds of smoke. The sun will become dark, and the moon will become as red as blood before the terrifying day of the Lord comes. Then whoever calls on the name of the Lord will be saved.* (Acts 2:17–21 GW)

The Right to Be a Saint

What Is a Saint?

The English meanings of the word *saint* are varied. First, it means: someone who has died and is honored by the church as a *Saint*. Second, it means: anyone who has died and gone to heaven. Third, it means: a person who is holy. Fourth, it means: someone who is exceptionally kind or long-suffering in coping with a difficult person.

Now let's see the meaning of the word *saint* from the Scriptures. The word means: a sacred (holy) one, a consecrated or dedicated person, or His pious (devout) one. Also, it means: to be set apart for God, to be exclusively His, to be made holy through the power of the Holy Spirit. Thus, by implication, it means those who are partakers of salvation in the kingdom of God.

Being a Saint

Is it possible to be a saint? From the meanings above, we say, "Yes." In fact, we are a saint if we are a true Christian. We do not have to die to be a saint because God calls us a saint **before** we die, **when** we die, and **after** we die (as we will see in the Scriptures that follow).

God calls us saints **before** we die in the following Psalms:

> As for the saints who are on the earth,
> "They are the excellent ones, in whom is all my delight." (Psalms 16:3)

Praise the LORD!
Sing to the LORD a new song,
And His praise in the assembly of saints.
(Psalm 149:1)

Also, God calls *all* His beloved in Rome *saints* in the literal translation of Romans 1:7, *"To all who are in Rome, beloved of God, called saints . . ." (YLT).*

Furthermore, the Holy Spirit makes intercession for *all* of God's children, not just a special few. In other words, *all* of God's children are called saints and the Holy Spirit makes intercession for *all* of us. *". . . He makes intercession for the saints according to the will of God"* (Romans 8:27).

We also see that the message of the Christian faith is delivered to *all* believers (our common salvation), not just a few especially holy ones.

> *Beloved, while I was very diligent to write to you concerning our common salvation, I found it necessary to write to you exhorting you to contend earnestly for the faith which was once for all delivered to the saints. (Jude 1:3)*

In the following verse, God calls us saints **when** we die: *"Precious in the sight of the LORD is the death of his saints"* (Psalm 116:15 KJV).

We are also called saints **after** we die since the dead in Christ are called *saints* throughout the book of Revelation and in many other places in the Bible.

> *And the graves were opened; and many bodies of the saints who had fallen asleep were raised;*

and coming out of the graves after His resurrection, they went into the holy city and appeared to many. (Matthew 27:52–53)

What Do Saints Do?

Here are just a few of the things the Scriptures show the saints doing:

1. Loving the Lord (Psalm 31:23)

2. Fearing the Lord (Psalm 34:9)

3. Hating evil (Psalm 97:10)

4. Performing righteous acts (Revelation 19:8)

5. Shouting for joy (Psalm 139:2)

6. Singing praise and giving thanks (Psalm 30:4)

7. Receiving and possessing the kingdom (Daniel 7:18)

8. Returning with Jesus when He comes again (Jude 1:14)

We Are Saints

We have a right to be a saint because of Jesus' work on the cross. If we have received Jesus as our Savior, then we are a saint. However, in today's culture, it would be best not to give ourselves the title of *"Saint____"* [fill in your name]—since many, if not most, would not understand. And we do not want to place any unnecessary obstacle before others. *". . . make up your mind not to put any stumbling block or obstacle in your brother's way"* (Romans 14:13 NIV).

The Right to Sleep in Peace

Sleep

Sleep is an absolute necessity for a healthy life. In the days ahead, being able to sleep peacefully is going to become more and more important. Why will it be so important? Because peoples' hearts will be failing them on account of fear and for what is coming upon the earth. Jesus warned us about these days we are living in now in Luke 21:25–26:

> *And there will be signs in the sun, in the moon, and in the stars; and on the earth distress of nations, with perplexity, the sea and the waves roaring; men's hearts failing them from fear and the expectation of those things which are coming on the earth, for the powers of the heavens will be shaken.*

Isaiah also prophesied about the deep darkness coming upon the world and the contrasting glory upon God's people:

> *For behold, the darkness shall cover the earth,*
> *And deep darkness the people;*
> *But the LORD will arise over you,*
> *And His glory will be seen upon you.*
> *(Isaiah 60:2)*

Those who only see the darkness will have a hard time sleeping compared to those seeing the coming glory.

Those Who Can Sleep in Peace

Those who know the Lord will keep them safe can sleep in peace. We see this in Psalm 4:8, *"I fall asleep in peace the moment I lie down because you alone, O LORD, enable me to live securely"* (GW).

Proverbs 3:24–26 also shows us the same thing—that we can have a good night's sleep because God keeps us safe and sound:

> *You'll take afternoon naps without a worry, you'll enjoy a good night's sleep. . . . Because GOD will be right there with you; he'll keep you safe and sound.* (TMSG)

Also, we can sleep in peace because we know that God is not sleeping but is always watching over us. *"He won't let you stumble, your Guardian God won't fall asleep. Not on your life!" . . . (Psalm 121:3–4 TMSG).*

Finally, we see that those who work for a living can expect to have a sweet sleep according to Ecclesiastes 5:12:

> *The sleep of working people is sweet, whether they eat a little or a lot. But the full stomachs that rich people have will not allow them to sleep.* (GW)

Too Much Sleep

Too much sleep is not good for us:

> *Don't be too fond of sleep; you'll end up in the poorhouse. Wake up and get up; then there'll be food on the table.* (Proverbs 20:13 TMSG)

We also see poverty linked to too much sleep in Proverbs 6:9–11:

> *How long will you lie there, you sluggard?*
>   *When will you get up from your sleep?*
> *A little sleep, a little slumber,*
>   *a little folding of the hands to rest—*
> *and poverty will come on you like a bandit*
>   *and scarcity like an armed man. (NIV)*

In addition, being lazy causes us to want to sleep even more. *"Laziness casts one into a deep sleep . . ." (Proverbs 19:15).*

What God Does When We Sleep

God uses our sleep to rejuvenate our bodies and for other reasons as stated in Job 33:14–18:

> *For God does speak—now one way,*
>   *now another—*
> *though man may not perceive it.*
> *In a dream, in a vision of the night,*
>   *when deep sleep falls on men*
>   *as they slumber in their beds,*
> *he may speak in their ears*
>   *and terrify them with warnings,*
> *to turn man from wrongdoing*
>   *and keep him from pride,*
> *to preserve his soul from the pit,*
>   *his life from perishing by the sword. (NIV)*

If our minds and hearts are focused on what God is doing, then we can sleep in peace knowing that He is building His church and His kingdom through the things coming upon the earth.

The Right to Be Judged

What it Means to Be Judged

To be judged means to have someone assess, after consideration and thought, the quality of our life or our value; then they pronounce (mentally or outwardly) their opinion for or against us, which results in them wanting to either defend us or rebuke us. In other words, making a judgment is to decide whether a person deserves praise or reprimand, vindication or punishment; it is the acknowledging of the right or wrong in a person's life.

Why Would We Want to Be Judged?

When many of us think of God's judgment, we only think of it as condemnation, punishment, or damnation. However, that is only a small portion of God's judgment; therefore, we need God to transform our thoughts about His judgments so that our attitudes are in line with His Word. The Scriptures exalt God's judgments as something *greatly* to be desired, as more precious than gold and sweeter than honey.

> . . . *The judgments of the LORD are true and*
> *righteous altogether.*
> *More to be desired are they than gold,*
> *Yea, than much fine gold;*
> *Sweeter also than honey and the honeycomb.*
> *(Psalms 19:9–10)*

We should want God's judgments since they are so valuable and because we have our best friend as our

Judge. *". . . He [Jesus] who was ordained by God to be Judge of the living and the dead" (Acts 10:42).* What a great comfort it is to know that we have our best friend as our judge! Our best friend wants the best for us—His judgments are for our good—for building us up.

The Paradox

The meaning of the word *paradox* is: a seeming contradiction. We just looked at how we should greatly desire the Lord's judgments; now we will see how the Scriptures show that we should try to avoid the Lord's judgment—a paradox. So how can we avoid God's judgment? We can avoid judgment by applying 1 Corinthians 11:31: *"For if we would judge ourselves, we would not be judged."* Even so, since we are not very good at judging ourselves, we will still need God's judgment— for the Bible says, *"Who can understand his errors?"* (Psalm 19:12).

God wants us to judge ourselves so that He does not have to judge us. Certainly, He gives us time to straighten out our lives, but if we do not, then He will help us get our lives in order by His judgments. *"If we get this straight now, we won't have to be straightened out later on"* (1 Corinthians 11:31 TMSG).

The Lord wants to stir in us a greater desire for His judgments; and to stir in us a greater desire to judge ourselves, thus avoiding the Lord's judgment. We need God to judge us and we need to judge ourselves.

Rewards Are the Result of Judgment

The judgment day is so that God can reward us for our works. These rewards will be for doing what Jesus wanted us to do with our lives; however, if we just did our own thing, those works will burn up as 1 Corinthians 3:11–15 shows us:

> . . . *that foundation is Jesus Christ. People may build on this foundation with gold, silver, precious stones, wood, hay, or straw. The day will make what each one does clearly visible because fire will reveal it. That fire will determine what kind of work each person has done. If what a person has built survives, he will receive a reward. If his work is burned up, he will suffer the loss. However, he will be saved, though it will be like going through a fire. (GW)*

Remember, the judgments of God are very good for us. When Jesus spoke to the churches in Revelation chapters 2 and 3, He made several judgments; plus, He made several promises of rewards if they would respond to His judgments of what was good and bad. His judgments were meant for the good of every person in each church. In other words, without Jesus judging what was right and wrong in their lives, many of the people would not have known what to keep on doing or what to stop doing. But with Jesus' judgments, they knew what to do and what rewards they would receive for obeying Him. So it is with us, God's judgments give right direction to our lives.

Do We Have the Right to Judge?

Do we have the right to judge others? Do others have the right to judge us? These questions take us to another paradox in the Word of God: Jesus said not to judge others and He made us judges of others. Keep in mind that Psalms 119:160 says, *"The sum of Thy word is truth"* (*YLT*). The sum (the totality) of Scripture produces the full truth.

As we have all heard quoted many times, "Jesus said, 'judge not;'" however, we do not often hear that He also said to judge. Jesus said in Matthew 7:1, *"Judge not, that you be not judged."* Then He said in John 7:24, *"Do not judge according to appearance, but judge with righteous judgment."*

The Apostle Paul said in 1 Corinthians 2:15, *"But he who is spiritual judges all things, yet he himself is rightly judged by no one."* Then in 1 Corinthians 6:2–3 he said:

> . . . *if the world will be judged by you, are you unworthy to judge the smallest matters? Do you not know that we shall judge angels? How much more, things that pertain to this life?"*

According to these Scriptures, there are times we should judge and there are times that we should not judge. We all know that at times we have judged too quickly; and at other times, we have been too slow to judge. Even so, when we do judge, we are not to judge by appearances but make righteous (right) judgments. And while we are judging, we are to keep in mind that we ourselves will be judged in the same way that we judge others. James warns us about this in James 2:13, *"For merciless judgment will come to the one who has shown no mercy. Mercy triumphs over judgment"* (*ISV*). This fact alone should keep our judgments to a minimum, and those judgments should be filled with mercy.

The Right to Hope

What Is Hope?

In the Old Testament there are over a dozen Hebrew words translated as hope. It's through this variety of words that we get a fuller picture of what hope is. One of the most common words used means: a shelter or a place of refuge. As this relates to God, it shows why we hope in Him—because He is a refuge and shelter for us. Another commonly used word literally means: a cord or an attachment. This shows that we hope in God because we have an attachment to Him. Yet another Hebrew word used for hope means: something waited for. This shows the idea of a confidence in God to do what He promised.

To sum up these meanings, hope is: expectancy, trust, faith, confidence and anticipation for the thing we long for from God—whom we are connected to as our shelter and refuge.

The Importance of Hope

Hope plays a most vital role in our faith. *"Now faith is the substance of things hoped for . . ." (Hebrews 11:1).* If we have no hope, can we have faith? It appears that hope is required for the exercise of faith. The father of faith, Abraham, had to have *hope* in order to believe God to fulfill His promise:

> *Against all hope, Abraham in hope believed and so became the father of many nations, just*

as it had been said to him, "So shall your offspring be." (Romans 4:18 NIV)

We have faith in God because we have hope in Him. To say it another way, since we have hope in God, we willingly put our trust in Him. So faith is the first companion of hope, the second is love since faith, hope, and love are the three things that abide. *"And now abide faith, hope, love, these three; but the greatest of these is love" (1 Corinthians 13:13).*

Love is the greatest stimulus of our hope in God. The more we love God, the more hope we will have in Him; and when our love for God abides, our hope in God will abide.

What Hope Does for Us

Hope is an *anchor* for our soul! An anchor is a device that keeps an object in place, keeps it secure, and keeps it connected. Our hope does all of these things for our soul because our hope keeps our soul in the right place—securely connected to God. And as the infomercials like to say, "But wait, there's more!"

Hope is not only an anchor, but it also *enters* into the very presence of God:

> *This hope we have as an anchor of the soul, both sure and steadfast, and which enters the Presence behind the veil. (Hebrews 6:19)*

Another translation says it this way:

> *We who have run for our very lives to God have every reason to grab the promised hope with both hands and never let go. It's an*

unbreakable spiritual lifeline, reaching past all
appearances right to the very presence of God.
(Hebrews 6:18–19 TMSG)

Wow! Hope is breathtaking! It is one of the three abiding pillars of our lives; yet, hope does not seem to have the recognition that it deserves. We recognize faith is essential for pleasing God as Hebrews 11:6 says, *"And without faith it is impossible to please God . . ." (NIV);* and love is recognized as the greatest commandment (see Matthew 22:36–40)—but what about hope? Is it recognized for what it is? Because of this, hope will be emphasized throughout the rest of this book.

The Hope of the Gospel

The Scripture speaks of "the hope of the gospel" as one of the most important aspects of the gospel. Could it be that your greatest freedom will come when you fully embrace all of the hope of the gospel? The Scriptures state that you should not be moved away from hope, and to everyone, hope has been proclaimed:

> *If indeed you continue in the faith, grounded*
> *and steadfast, and are not moved away from*
> *the hope of the gospel which you heard, which*
> *was preached to every creature under*
> *heaven . . . (Colossians 1:23)*

Since the hope of the gospel is so important, we should know what it is. So what is the hope of the gospel? The hope of the gospel is like a diamond with many facets with each one giving more glory to the diamond. In light of this, in the next few chapters we will try to expose some of the many facets of the hope of the gospel—that hope is astonishingly beautiful!

The Right to Die in Peace

Death's Origin

Death means many different things to the diverse people groups around the world. However, for the Christians in every nation, tribe, tongue, and people, it should have the same basic meaning because we have one faith and one Lord—Jesus Christ. To say it another way, Christians have one truth (the Bible) for the basis of their view of death; thus, the Christian's view of death can be like God's viewpoint of death since He has much to say about death within the Bible.

Obviously, this does not mean that every culture will have the same customs concerning death; it simply means that every Christian of every culture should have the same *central* view of death, since our view of death is based upon the same Holy Scriptures.

Like all of the other rights in this book, our right to die in peace and our view of death should be based upon what God says within the Bible. Even so, since this book is not a detailed study of any of these areas, we will only be able to look briefly at the subject of death for a Christian.

Where did death come from? Death came because of sin. That is, Adam and Eve's sin brought death into the world, and we have all sinned; the wages of sin is death. *"The payment for sin is death . . ." (Romans 6:23 GW).*

What causes us to sin? Desire is the beginning of sin, which brings about the end of sin—death. The Apostle James explains this process in James 1:13–15:

Let no one say when he is tempted, "I am tempted by God"; for God cannot be tempted by evil, nor does He Himself tempt anyone. But each one is tempted when he is drawn away by his own desires and enticed. Then, when desire has conceived, it gives birth to sin; and sin, when it is full-grown, brings forth death.

The Fear of Death

We need to think about death the way Jesus thinks about death. He knew that the hope of the gospel would begin with death—His death.

By embracing death, taking it into himself, he destroyed the Devil's hold on death and freed all who cower through life, scared to death of death" (Hebrews 2:14–15 TMSG)

The hope of the gospel is what changes our view of death completely from the world's view of death because of what Jesus did for us on the cross. Through His death, we have one of the major facets of the hope of the gospel—***freedom from the fear of death.***

Fear of death causes us to be subject to the bondage of doing whatever it takes to preserve our lives instead of being most concerned about fulfilling God's will for our lives, regardless of the cost. In view of the fact that this is such a significant aspect of Jesus' work, I want to quote another translation of this same verse:

. . . that through death He might destroy him who had the power of death, that is, the devil, and release those who through fear of death

were all their lifetime subject to bondage.
(Hebrews 2:14–15)

The <u>Central</u> Hope of the Gospel

Without the hope of the gospel, there really is no gospel (good news). Therefore, we need to ask, "What is the central hope of the gospel?" The central hope of the gospel is ***eternal life with God:***

> . . . *a faith and knowledge resting on the hope of eternal life, which God, who does not lie, promised before the beginning of time. (Titus 1:2 NIV)*

What is eternal life? Eternal life is to know God the Father and His Son Jesus Christ personally by living together with them forever—what we call heaven. So how do we obtain this eternal life? It only comes from the Father through Jesus Christ as John 17:1–3 declares:

> *Jesus spoke these words, lifted up His eyes to heaven, and said: "Father, the hour has come. Glorify Your Son, that Your Son also may glorify You, as You have given Him authority over all flesh, that He should give eternal life to as many as You have given Him. And this is eternal life, that they may know You, the only true God, and Jesus Christ whom You have sent."*

This brings us to yet another major facet of the central hope of the gospel—***resurrection of the dead.*** Obviously, there is no hope of eternal life if there is no resurrection of the dead. We see this clearly in 1 Corinthians 15:13–20:

> *If the dead can't be brought back to life, then Christ hasn't come back to life. If Christ hasn't come back to life, our message has no meaning and your faith also has no meaning. And we are obviously witnesses who lied about God because we testified that he brought Christ back to life. But if it's true that the dead don't come back to life, then God didn't bring Christ back to life. Certainly, if the dead don't come back to life, then Christ hasn't come back to life either. If Christ hasn't come back to life, your faith is worthless and sin still has you in its power. Then those who have died as believers in Christ no longer exist. If Christ is our hope in this life only, we deserve more pity than any other people. But now Christ has come back from the dead. He is the very first person of those who have died to come back to life. (GW)*

The hope of the gospel is that God will raise the dead—death is not the end of our existence but the beginning of life for the Christian in the very presence of God!

> *I have hope in God, which they themselves also accept, that there will be a resurrection of the dead, both of the just and the unjust. (Acts 24:15)*

Another facet of the hope of the gospel is **the second coming of Jesus to this earth.** Jesus said, "*And if I go and prepare a place for you, I will come again and* receive you to Myself . . ." *(John 14:3)*. Titus 2:13 also speaks of the wonderful hope of Jesus returning to the earth:

> *Looking for that blessed hope, and the glorious appearing of the great God and our Saviour Jesus Christ. (KJV)*

Yet another facet of the hope of the gospel is that **we will have a glorified body like Jesus' body:**

> *Beloved, now we are children of God; and it has not yet been revealed what we shall be, but we know that when He is revealed, we shall be like Him . . . (1 John 3:2)*

One portion of the Bible that is devoted to what our glorified body will be like is 1 Corinthians 15:35–58. However, since this passage of Scripture is too long to quote in its entirety in this book, we will only be able to cite a few of those verses here.

> *But someone will say, "How are the dead raised up? And with what body do they come?" (1 Corinthians 15:35)*
>
> *It is sown a natural body, it is raised a spiritual body. There is a natural body, and there is a spiritual body. (1 Corinthians 15:44)*
>
> *And as we have borne the image of the man of dust, we shall also bear the image of the heavenly Man [Jesus]. (1 Corinthians 15:49)*

Today's final facet of the hope of the gospel is that **we will experience and share in God's glory.**

> *... Christ is in you, therefore you can look forward to sharing in God's glory. It's that simple. That is the substance of our Message. (Colossians 1:27 TMSG)*

Should We Want to Die?

Should we want to die since we have such a great hope? The answer is both "yes" and "no." It is Scriptural not to want to die and also to want to die. Paul said it best in Philippians 1:21–26:

> *For to me, to live is Christ and to die is gain. If I am to go on living in the body, this will mean fruitful labor for me. Yet what shall I choose? I do not know! I am torn between the two: I desire to depart and be with Christ, which is better by far; but it is more necessary for you that I remain in the body. Convinced of this, I know that I will remain, and I will continue with all of you for your progress and joy in the faith. (NIV)*

We should not want to die prematurely, that is, before we have finished our "race;" but when our work is finished on this earth, we will doubtless welcome death because of the hope of the gospel that we have living within us. Paul says in 2 Timothy 4:6–8:

> *... the time of my departure is at hand. I have fought the good fight, I have finished the race, I have kept the faith. Finally, there is laid up for me the crown of righteousness, which the Lord, the righteous Judge, will give to me on that*

Day, and not to me only but also to all who have loved His appearing.

We have the right to die in *peace* because we have the central hope of the gospel—eternal life with God. In the next chapters, we will continue to see more facets of the hope of the gospel.

The Right to Escape the Second Death

More Facets of Our Hope

We ended the last chapter with 2 Timothy 4:8:

> *Finally, there is laid up for me the crown of righteousness, which the Lord, the righteous Judge, will give to me on that Day, and not to me only but also to all who have loved His appearing.*

This verse gives us another facet of the hope of the gospel—***our eternal rewards,*** including crowns. There are many different kinds of rewards; crowns are mentioned as just one type of reward. The crown of life is spoken of in James 1:12 and Revelation 2:10, and the crown of glory in 1 Peter 5:4.

We will be surprised with the rewards we receive since Jesus, by the Holy Spirit, produced the fruit in us. In fact, Jesus in us *is* our hope of any glory. In other words, we will be rewarded in heaven to the extent we allowed Jesus to live His life through us.

> *I have been crucified with Christ; it is no longer I who live, but Christ lives in me; and the life which I now live in the flesh I live by faith in the Son of God, who loved me and gave Himself for me. (Galatians 2:20)*

The Second Death

We all know that death is a part of life because we will all die (unless we are alive when Jesus returns—see 1 Corinthians 15:51–52). Why will we die? It's because God has appointed us to die *once* as we see in Hebrews 9:27, *"And as it is appointed for men to die once, but after this the judgment."* We are appointed to die only *once*. Why would God say that? Is it even possible to die more than once? Yes it is; the first death is physical; the second death is spiritual and eternal.

We all need to know that the Scriptures speak of a *second* death and that God does not want us to be a part of it. We can begin to see the seriousness of this particular fact of the gospel in 1 Peter 4:18, *"If the righteous one is scarcely saved, where will the ungodly and the sinner appear?"*

The word *scarcely* in the above verse means: with difficulty or with much work we are saved. So then, as the verse states, *"where will the ungodly and the sinner appear?"* To say it another way, "What will become of the ungodly and the sinner since we are scarcely saved?" The answer is that they will die a second death as Revelation 20:13–15 shows:

> *The sea gave up the dead that were in it, and death and Hades gave up the dead that were in them, and each person was judged according to what he had done. Then death and Hades were thrown into the lake of fire. The lake of fire is the second death. If anyone's name was not found written in the book of life, he was thrown into the lake of fire. (NIV)*

This shows us two more facets of the hope of the gospel—**our names written in the Book of Life** and **escaping the second death.** The second death is the worst death possible since it is spiritual and eternal; it is eternal separation from God in the lake of fire. The only way to escape the second death is to have our names written in the Book of Life.

The Final Judgment

The final judgment mentioned above in Revelation 20 takes place after the first resurrection. If we are part of the first resurrection, then the second death has no power over us. Plus, those who are part of the first resurrection will reign with Christ for one thousand years.

> *Blessed and holy are those who have part in the first resurrection. The second death has no power over them, but they will be priests of God and of Christ and will reign with him for a thousand years. (Revelation 20:6 NIV)*

We do not have to fear the judgments of God *if* we have our name in the Book of Life. That does not mean that we will not be judged because we shall all stand before the judgment seat of Christ to give an account of ourselves to God:

> *For we must all appear before the judgment seat of Christ, that each one may receive the things done in the body, according to what he has done, whether good or bad. (2 Corinthians 5:9–10)*

The judgments of God are very important to us because they determine our eternal destiny.

> *He who is unjust, let him be unjust still; he who is filthy, let him be filthy still; he who is righteous, let him be righteous still; he who is holy, let him be holy still. (Revelation 22:11)*

If we are already free from sin in Christ, then our physical death releases us to total freedom in Christ. However, if a person is bound in sin, not knowing Jesus as Savior, then that person will have a first death and a second death—experiencing total bondage and eternal dying.

The Bible encourages us to live totally in Christ now so we will not be ashamed when He appears but be confident in our relationship with Christ knowing that He is our salvation.

> *And now, children, stay with Christ. Live deeply in Christ. Then we'll be ready for him when he appears, ready to receive him with open arms, with no cause for red-faced guilt or lame excuses when he arrives. (1 John 2:28 TMSG)*

We have the hope of the gospel, which includes having our names written in the Book of Life. Therefore, we will not be hurt by the second death!

Day 30

The Right to Experience Total Restoration

Restoration

Another hope of the gospel is **the restoration of all things.** The Scriptures tell us that not *all* things will be restored *until* Jesus Christ returns to earth:

> *And that He may send Jesus Christ, who was preached to you before, whom heaven must receive until the times of restoration of all things, which God has spoken by the mouth of all His holy prophets since the world began. (Acts 3:20–21)*

The restoration of all things is the hope of the gospel. Restoration means to restore something to an earlier condition or to a better condition. In this case, it means to restore to an even better condition than before mankind fell into sin. Isaiah shows us some of the restoration that Jesus will bring when He comes again:

> *Wolves will live with lambs.*
> *Leopards will lie down with goats.*
> *Calves, young lions, and year-old lambs will be together, and little children will lead them.*
> *Cows and bears will eat together.*
> *Their young will lie down together.*
> *Lions will eat straw like oxen.*
> *Infants will play near cobras' holes.*

Toddlers will put their hands into vipers' nests.
They will not hurt or destroy anyone anywhere
    on my holy mountain.
The world will be filled with the knowledge of
    the LORD like water covering the sea.
(Isaiah 11:6–9 GW)

One of the major themes in the Bible from the time of the fall of man into sin to the end of the Book of Revelation is restoration. The Bible shows that God is the One who will restore all things; even if He uses mankind, it is still His power working through them.

The ultimate restoration is God the Father coming to live on the earth, which will make the restored condition even better than the first condition of the earth before humanity sinned.

This restoration has, is, and will take place in stages. Remember, for thousands of years God through the prophets prepared humanity for the first coming of Jesus; then when Jesus came, He prepared humanity for the coming of the Holy Spirit, then went back to heaven. Now the Holy Spirit's work through us is preparing the world for the second coming of Jesus. Then when Jesus comes a second time, He Himself, the Holy Spirit, and all God's people will have one thousand years to prepare everything for the coming of God the Father to live on the new earth.

The New Heavens and the New Earth

Many speak of the end of the world as the end of life on earth and the end of the earth itself. However, the Bible speaks of life continuing on earth even though the earth as we know it will be destroyed because God is making a new heavens and a new earth for us to live on eternally.

> *"For as the new heavens and the new earth which I will make shall remain before Me," says the LORD, "So shall your descendants and your name remain." (Isaiah 66:22)*

The Apostle Peter also speaks of God making a new heavens and a new earth where righteous people will live:

> *Nevertheless we, according to His promise, look for new heavens and a new earth in which righteousness dwells. (2 Peter 3:13)*

This is another facet of the great hope of the gospel— **the new heavens and the new earth in which righteousness dwells.**

God the Father Will Come to Earth

Another facet of the hope of the gospel that we mentioned briefly is **God living on the earth with us.** At that time, the Father, the Son, and the Holy Spirit will live with us in His holy city—the New Jerusalem! This wonderful news is in Revelation 21:1–4:

> *Then I saw a new heaven and a new earth, because the first heaven and the first earth had disappeared, and the sea was gone. I also saw the holy city, New Jerusalem, coming down from God out of heaven, prepared like a bride adorned for her husband. I heard a loud voice from the throne say, "See, the tabernacle of God is among humans! He will make his home*

with them, and they will be his people. God himself will be with them, and he will be their God. He will wipe every tear from their eyes. There won't be death anymore. There won't be any grief, crying, or pain, because the first things have disappeared." (ISV)

The Bride of Christ

Another astonishing facet of the hope of the gospel is that ***we can be Jesus' bride:***

Let us be glad and rejoice and give him glory, for the marriage of the Lamb has come; and His wife has made herself ready. And to her it was granted to be arrayed in fine linen, clean and bright, for the fine linen is the righteous acts of the saints. (Revelation 19:7–8)

When John sees Jesus' wife, he sees the holy city:

"Come! I will show you the bride, the wife of the lamb." He carried me away in the Spirit to a large, high mountain and showed me the holy city, Jerusalem, coming down from God out of heaven. (Revelation 21:9 ISV)

The size of God's holy city is staggering; according to many, it is about 1400 (some say 1500) miles long, wide, and high! It could mean that the city is over 1,960,000 square miles on *each* level of the city (assuming the city has levels or tiers) and these levels extend about 1400 miles high. This could mean that there are thousands of levels in the city. In other words, the New Jerusalem is mind-bogglingly huge—it is gargantuan beyond our current comprehension!

> *The city was square: its length was the same as its width. He measured the city with his rod, and it was 12,000 stadia long. Its length, width, and height were the same. (Revelation 21:16 ISV)*

In Christ, we have the right to experience this total restoration—to dwell eternally with God in His holy city, which is another facet of the hope of the gospel—***to dwell in the holy city of God with all its pleasures.*** These pleasures include seeing God's face!—and never experiencing nighttime again because we will be continually experiencing the light of God.

> *The throne of God and the lamb will be in the city. His servants will worship him and see his face. His name will be on their foreheads. There will be no more night, and they will not need any light from lamps or the sun because the Lord God will shine on them. They will rule as kings forever and ever. (Revelation 22:3–5 GW)*

When we have the hope of the gospel in all of its facets, it increases our desire for Jesus to come and restore all things as soon as possible.

> *He who testifies to these things says, "Yes, I am coming soon." Amen. Come, Lord Jesus. (Revelation 22:20).*

Day 31

The Right to Proclaim the Gospel

The Good News

In light of the fact that the word *gospel* means "good news," and since most of the news the world hears daily is bad news, this is a wonderful time to proclaim the gospel! But what does that mean? It means to proclaim the good news that the kingdom of God has come and is coming, which means that **the King** is coming again.

The King Is Coming

Another facet of the hope of the gospel we have the right to proclaim is that ***Jesus is coming as King!*** Since Jesus is the eternal King, He was King when He came to earth the first time; however, He did not take on the form of a king but came as a suffering servant not operating as a king would. People even had to ask if Jesus was a king because He did not appear to be a king.

> *Pilate therefore said to Him, "Are You a king then?" Jesus answered, "You say rightly that I am a king. For this cause I was born, and for this cause I have come into the world . . ." (John 18:37)*

Jesus was, is, and will always be King as we see in Psalm 10:16, *"The LORD is King forever and ever . . ."* Jesus is not just a king, He is the King of kings—the King of every king that ever shall be. *"And He has on His robe* and on His thigh a name written: KING OF KINGS AND LORD OF LORDS" (Revelation 19:16).

He Is Coming to Rule

Jesus will come to the earth again as King of all the earth and everything will be subjected to Him—He will rule with a rod of iron:

> "Yet I have set My King
> On My holy hill of Zion."

> "I will declare the decree:
> The LORD has said to Me,
> 'You are My Son,
> Today I have begotten You.
> Ask of Me, and I will give You
> The nations for Your inheritance,
> And the ends of the earth for Your possession.
> You shall break them with a rod of iron;
> You shall dash them to pieces like a potter's
>   vessel.'"
> (Psalm 2:6–9)

Some of the greatest news we can proclaim is that the King is coming to take charge—to establish His kingdom upon the earth. However, this does not mean that He is not already establishing His kingdom upon the earth to a degree. What it does mean is that there is a much greater manifestation of His kingdom coming in the future when the King Himself comes to earth again:

> Out of his mouth comes a sharp sword with which to strike down the nations. "He will rule them with an iron scepter." (Revelation 19:15 NIV)

Our Commission

We have the right to be a missionary—one who proclaims the gospel and makes disciples of Jesus. When Jesus said to go into all the world, it applies geographically and to all areas of society. There are seven major spheres of society that the Lord wants us to go into: arts and entertainment, media, business, government, education, family, and religion. Jesus gives us the authority to proclaim Him in all these areas of society, and the entire world geographically. *"And He said to them, 'Go into all the world and preach the gospel to every creature.'" (Mark 16:15).* Plus, in Matthew 28:18–20 Jesus declares:

> *All authority has been given to Me in heaven and on earth. Go therefore and make disciples of all the nations, baptizing them in the name of the Father and of the Son and of the Holy Spirit, teaching them to observe all things that I have commanded you; and lo, I am with you always, even to the end of the age. Amen.*

Notice that we are to make disciples, not just converts to Christianity. We make disciples by teaching them to observe everything Jesus commanded, which enables them to live in the kingdom of God *now*—while proclaiming that the kingdom of God is yet to come. Both are true—the kingdom of God is here and it is yet to come.

What the King Will Be Looking For

The King will be looking for the same things in every nation and He will separate nations based upon those things:

When the Son of Man comes in His glory . . . All the nations will be gathered before Him . . . Then the King will say to those on His right hand, "Come, you blessed of My Father, inherit the kingdom prepared for you from the foundation of the world: for I was hungry and you gave Me food; I was thirsty and you gave Me drink; I was a stranger and you took Me in; I was naked and you clothed Me; I was sick and you visited Me; I was in prison and you came to Me."

Then the righteous will answer Him, saying, "Lord, when did we see You hungry and feed You, or thirsty and give You drink? When did we see You a stranger and take You in, or naked and clothe You? Or when did we see You sick, or in prison, and come to You?" And the King will answer and say to them, "Assuredly, I say to you, inasmuch as you did it to one of the least of these My brethren, you did it to Me." (Matthew 25:31–40)

There will be a time when we will no longer proclaim that King Jesus is coming because He will already be here on earth! However, until then, we have the right to proclaim the good news that the King is coming to reign on the earth.

Conclusion

The Right to Fight

We have the right to fight for our rights and we must! However, our fight is not with flesh and blood but against principalities and powers; therefore, God gives us His power to fight these forces so we can win the victory. 2 Corinthians 10:3–5 states:

> *For though we live in the world, we do not wage war as the world does. The weapons we fight with are not the weapons of the world. On the contrary, they have divine power to demolish strongholds. We demolish arguments and every pretension that sets itself up against the knowledge of God, and we take captive every thought to make it obedient to Christ. (NIV)*

God Thinks About You

In conclusion to this book, I want to share a couple of Scriptures that speak of God thinking about you. As you know, when you really love a person, you will think about them often. Hopefully this book has helped your love for God to increase and thus your thoughts about Him to increase.

The main thing I want to leave you with is the fact of how much God loves you—He has thoughts about you all the time! This wonderful fact is hard to imagine (that the God of the universe is thinking about *you* all the time!). Even so, you can believe that it is true because God says it in His Word. He says that His thoughts about you are more in number than the grains of sand! God tells you this amazing fact in Psalm 139:17–18:

> *How precious are your thoughts concerning*
> *   me, O God!*
> *How vast in number they are!*
> *If I try to count them, there would be more of*
> *   them than there are grains of sand . . . (GW)*

Wow! Wow! Wow! God thinks about **you** so often! How wonderful it is to know that; but wouldn't it also be great to know the kind of thoughts that He has about you? Yes, and God tells you what His thoughts about you are—good thoughts, hopeful thoughts:

> *For I know the thoughts that I think toward*
> *you, says the LORD, thoughts of peace and not*
> *of evil, to give you a future and a hope.*
> *(Jeremiah 29:11)*

What Now?

Remember, you are in a relationship with God. A relationship flows two ways. You have seen some of God's part of the relationship in the verses quoted above; the next two verses of Jeremiah 29 show you some of your part of the relationship—the "What now?" for you:

> *Then you will call upon Me and go and pray to*
> *   Me, and I will listen to you.*
> *And you will seek Me and find Me, when you*
> *   search for Me with all your heart.*
> *(Jeremiah 29:12–13)*

Author Steven J. Campbell may be contacted at his
personal email:

stevecamp3@hotmail.com

Join us on Facebook:

www.facebook.com/StevenJCampbellBooks

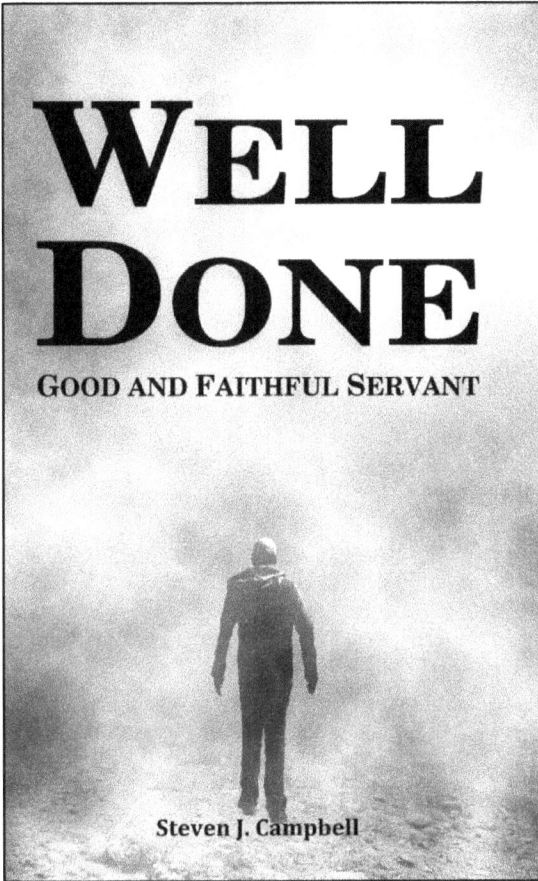

Well Done
Good and Faithful Servant

by Steven J. Campbell

This book is for helping you to fulfill your purpose in the great end-time harvest and to hear Jesus say to you, "Well done."

Steven J. Campbell

I Am Born Again,

Now What?

An Invitation to Grow in Christ

I am Born Again,
Now What?

An Invitation to Grow in Christ

by Steven J. Campbell
and
Austin J. Campbell

This book is about growing in Christ in the basics of Christianity, helping you to experience His love in a greater measure.

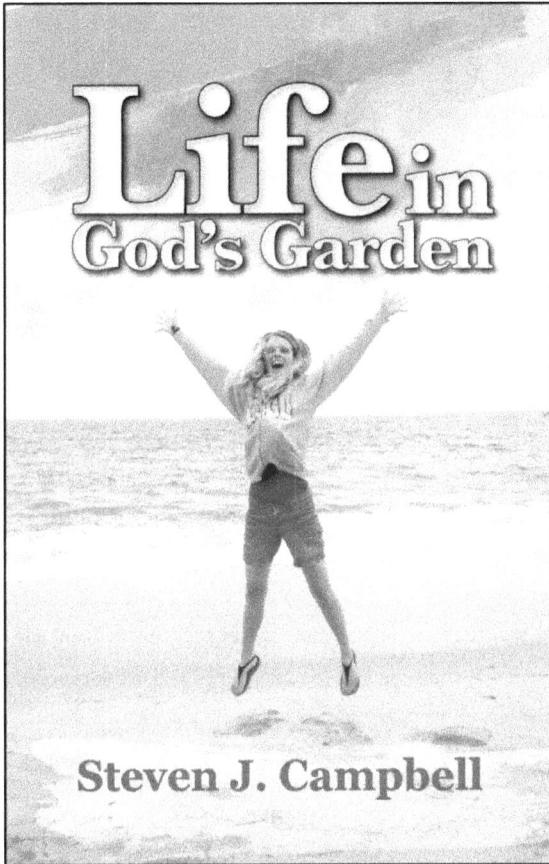

Life in God's Garden

by Steven J. Campbell
and
Austin J. Campbell

*This book is about how we are created to
live in a garden-type reality and experience
life in all its fullness.*

www.ingramcontent.com/pod-product-compliance
Lightning Source LLC
Chambersburg PA
CBHW071054040426
42443CB00013B/3332